AA004088

VISUAL 2016

The First International Conference on Applications and Systems of Visual Paradigms

November 13 - 17, 2016

Barcelona, Spain

VISUAL 2016 Editors

Vijayan Asari, University of Dayton, USA

Claus-Peter Rückemann, Leibniz Universität Hannover / Westfälische Wilhelms-Universität Münster / North-German Supercomputing Alliance (HLRN), Germany

Printed from e-media with permission by:

Curran Associates, Inc.
57 Morehouse Lane
Red Hook, NY 12571

Some format issues inherent in the e-media version may also appear in this print version.

Printed by Curran Associates, Inc. (2016)

International Academy, Research, and Industry Association (IARIA)
412 Derby Way
Wilmington, DE 19810

Phone: (408) 893-6407
Fax: (408) 527-6351

petre@iaria.org

Additional copies of this publication are available from:

Curran Associates, Inc.
57 Morehouse Lane
Red Hook, NY 12571 USA
Phone: 845-758-0400
Fax: 845-758-2633
Email: curran@proceedings.com
Web: www.proceedings.com

Table of Contents

Ontology-Based Modelling of Sensor and Data Processing Ressources Using OWL 1
Denis Smirnov and Peter Stutz

Selecting Adequate Aerial Perceptual Functions with Fuzzy Logic 8
Christian Hellert and Peter Stutz

Local Edge/Corner Feature Integration for Illumination Invariant Face Recognition 13
Almabrok Essa and Vijayan Asari

Approximating Imprecise Planar Tesselations with Voronoi Diagrams 19
Narciso Javier Aguilera Centeno, Belen Palop del Rio, and Hebert Perez-Roses

Incremental Reconstruction of Moving Object Trajectory 24
Muhammad Majid Afzal, Karim Ouazzane, Vassil Vassilev, and Yogesh Patel

A Fast Audiovisual Attention Model for Human Detection and Localization on a Companion Robot 30
Remi Ratajczak, Denis Pellerin, Catherine Garbay, and Quentin Labourey

A Method of Object Identification Based on Sea Image Processing 36
Jing Zhang, Shaoyan Rao, and Tianchi Zhang

Visual Public Protection Disaster Relief and Critical Infrastructure 41
Aurel Machalek, Dominc Dunlop, Carlo Simon, and Ralf Hoben

Full Incremental Learning for Along Classification of Textual Images 45
Vincent Poulain d'Andecy, Aurelie Joseph, and Saddok Kebairi

Enhanced Hash-based Intra Block Copy for HEVC Screen Content Coding using Sucessive Elimination Algorithm 50
Ilseung Kim and Jechang Jeong

Research on Optimization Technology of Three Dimensional Model 55
Jing Zhang, Bowen Li, and Tianchi Zhang

VISUAL 2016

Foreword

The First International Conference on Applications and Systems of Visual Paradigms (VISUAL 2016), held between November 13-17, 2016 - Barcelona, Spain was an inaugural event in putting together complementary domains were visual approaches are considered in a synergetic view.

Visual paradigms were developed on the basis of understanding the brain's and eye's functions. They spread over computation, environment representation, autonomous devices, data presentation, and software/hardware approaches. The advent of Big Data, high speed images/camera, complexity and ubiquity of applications and services raises several requests on integrating visual-based solutions in cross-domain applications.

We take here the opportunity to warmly thank all the members of the VISUAL 2016 Technical Program Committee, as well as the numerous reviewers. The creation of such a high quality conference program would not have been possible without their involvement. We also kindly thank all the authors who dedicated much of their time and efforts to contribute to VISUAL 2016. We truly believe that, thanks to all these efforts, the final conference program consisted of top quality contributions.

Also, this event could not have been a reality without the support of many individuals, organizations, and sponsors. We are grateful to the members of the VISUAL 2016 organizing committee for their help in handling the logistics and for their work to make this professional meeting a success.

We hope that VISUAL 2016 was a successful international forum for the exchange of ideas and results between academia and industry and for the promotion of progress in the area of visual oriented technologies.

We are convinced that the participants found the event useful and communications very open. We also hope the attendees enjoyed the charm of Barcelona, Spain.

VISUAL 2016 Chairs:

VISUAL 2016 Advisory Committee

Vijayan Asari, University of Dayton, USA
Robert S. Laramee, Swansea University, UK
Mark A. Whiting, Pacific Northwest National Laboratory, Richland, USA

VISUAL 2016

Committee

VISUAL 2016 Advisory Committee

Vijayan Asari, University of Dayton, USA
Robert S. Laramee, Swansea University, UK
Mark A. Whiting, Pacific Northwest National Laboratory, Richland, USA

VISUAL 2016 Technical Program Committee

Driss Aboutajdine, CNRST - Centre National de Coordination et de Plantification de la Recherche Scientifique et Technique, Rabat, Morocco
Vijayan Asari, University of Dayton, USA
Oscar Kin-Chung Au, School of Creative Media - City University of Hong Kong, Hong Kong
George Baciu, The Hong Kong Polytechnic University, Hong Kong
Jenny Benois-Pineau, University of Bordeaux, France
Stefano Berretti, University of Firenze, Italy
Hans-Peter Bischof, Rochester Institute of Technology, USA
Kadi Bouatouch, IRISA, University of Rennes 1, France
Miguel Ceriani, Sapienza University of Rome, Italy
Sabine Coquillart, INRIA Grenoble Rhône-Alpes, France
Mohamed Daoudi, Telecom Lille/ CRIStAL (UMR 9189), France
Francois Destelle, Insight: Centre for Data Analytics | Dublin City University, Ireland
Dominik Endres, Philipps-University Marburg, Germany
Andrew Fish, University of Brighton, UK
Denis Gracanin, Virginia Tech, USA
Miguel Angel Guevara Lopez, University of Minho, Portugal
Kun Guo, School of Psychology | University of Lincoln, UK
Luis Gustavo Nonato, University of Sao Paulo at Sao Carlos, Brazil
Naohisa Hashimoto, National Institute of Advanced Industrial Science and Technology, Japan
Martin Kampel, Vienna University of Technology, Austria
Giannis Karaseitanidis, Institute of Communication and Computer Systems, Greece
Gunta Krumina, University of Latvia, Latvia
Robert S. Laramee, Swansea University, UK
Sven Linker, University of Brighton, UK
Zhanping Liu, Kentucky State University, USA
Célia Martinie, ICS-IRIT | University Toulouse 3 Paul Sabatier, France
Kresimir Matkovic, VRVis Research Center, Vienna, Austria
Thomas Moeslund, Aalborg University, Denmark
Sudhir Mudur, Concordia University, Canada
Laurent Nana, Université Bretagne Occidentale, France
Nicoletta Noceti, University of Genova, Italy
Klimis Ntalianis, Athens University of Applied Sciences, Greece

Vincent Poulain d'Andecy, ITESOFT, France
Isaac Rudomin, Barcelona Supercomputer Center, Spain
Filip Sadlo, Heidelberg University, Germany
Kristian Sandberg, Computational Solutions, Inc., USA
Nickolas S. Sapidis, University of Western Macedonia, Greece
João Saraiva, HASLab/INESC TEC & University of Minho, Portugal
Jacob Scharcanski, Instituto de Informatica | UFRGS - Universidade Federal do Rio Grande do Sul, Brazil
Sonja Schimmler, Universitaet der Bundeswehr Muenchen, Germany
Siniša Šegvić, University of Zagreb, Croatia
Gurjot Singh, Fairleigh Dickinson University, New Jersey, USA
Luciano Soares, Insper Instituto de Ensino e Pesquisa, Brazil
Ahmet Soylu, Norwegian University of Science and Technology (NTNU), Norway
Gem Stapleton, University of Brighton, UK
Jun Tao, University of Notre Dame, USA
João Manuel R. S. Tavares, Faculdade de Engenharia da Universidade do Porto, Portugal
Alex Wade, Birmingham City University, UK
Hazem Wannous, CRIStAL Lab. UMR CNRS 9189 - University Lille 1 / Telecom Lille, France
Mark A. Whiting, Pacific Northwest National Laboratory, Richland, USA
Arnold J. Wilkins, University of Essex, UK
Sai-Keung Wong, National Chiao Tung University, Taiwan
Pengcheng Xi, National Research Council, Canada
Wei Xu, Brookhaven National Laboratory / Stony Brook University, USA
Mohammed Yeasin, University of Memphis, USA

Copyright Information

Ontology-Based Modelling of Sensor and Data Processing Ressources Using OWL

A Proof of Concept

Denis Smirnov and Peter Stütz
Institute of Flight Systems
University of the Bundeswehr Munich
Neubiberg, Germany
e-mail: denis.smirnov@unibw.de, peter.stuetz@unibw.de

Abstract—**In this paper, we describe an ontology-based system to inventory and model installed sensor and respective data processing resources on-board airborne surveillance aircrafts. The algorithms are packaged and described in form of discrete processing modules, each representing a low level image processing step. While the implementation of the algorithms is kept detached in a separate library, the description of modules and its parameters are stored in an ontology, representing a knowledge database using Web Ontology Language as a knowledge representation language. Based on the module description stored in the knowledge database, it is possible to identify and manage processing chains capable of solving complex image processing tasks.**

Keywords-Ontology; Web Ontology Language (OWL); Image Processing Management; Knowledge Management; sensor and data ressources.

I. INTRODUCTION

Presently we witness an increasing demand for highly automated deployment of heterogeneous sensors on-board unmanned aircraft, either to yield better environmental awareness in the context of collision free flight or, as in the given case, to conduct typical Intelligence, Surveillance & Reconnaissance (ISR) missions in a more automated fashion, thereby relying mostly on imaging sensors operating in various spectral regions. However in aviation space, power and processing resources are limited. Therefore it is necessary to work economically with resources and manage them in an intelligent way. Furthermore, the sensor data processing and evaluation on-board a flying platform takes place under changing circumstances for example resulting from changing position and orientation of the Unmanned Aerial Vehicle (UAV), varying lighting conditions and different surface backgrounds (e.g., rural, urban, maritime). To cope with this situation it is meaningful to have a wide set of different sensors and associated data processing algorithms, since there is no algorithm that performs in an adequate way in every situation. For a complex image processing task (e.g., vehicle- and person detection) there are several equal processing steps, which have to be executed for each task, e.g., preprocessing steps or region-of-interest (ROI) selection. When executing multiple tasks one can save resources and computational time reusing the processing steps, which are required repeatedly instead of starting the same algorithm multiple times. Thus, there is a need for a system that manages sensor resources and image processing capabilities in a meaningful way. The Institute of Flight Systems published several papers ([1]–[5]) on the topic of airborne sensor- and perception management. In this paper we now focus on the ontology based knowledge extension of the so called *Sensor and Perception Management System (S&PMS)*, first introduced in [4].

The S&PMS is best described as a three layer architecture to inventory relevant resources (e.g., sensors and image processing algorithms) and manage their usage as shown in Figure 1.

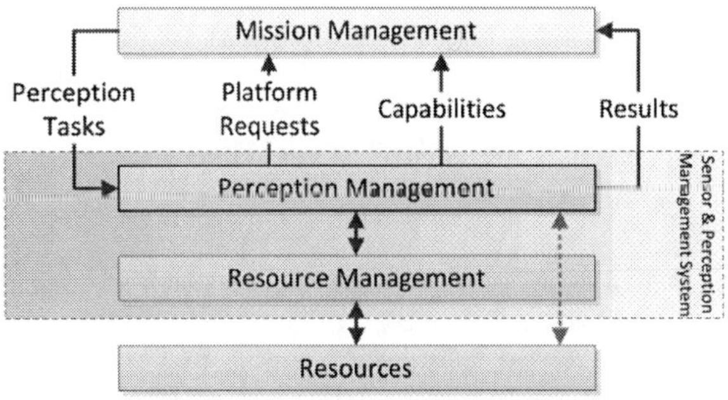

Figure 1. Three layer architecture of the Sensor and Perception Management System.

One of the S&PMS's key aspects is the module based approach to package image processing algorithms into perception modules. Each module fulfils a special low level image processing requirement, e.g., noise reduction or ROI. Modules are designed to be standalone or to be combined with different modules to solve a higher level image processing task (*perception task*), like vehicle detection within a given street segment. The combination of at least two low level modules or a sensor-module combination creates a *perception chain*. Eventually a considerable variety of different perceptions chains (redundant chains) results, which potentially solve the same perception task, based on the (sensor) configuration of the UAV and the available perception modules. This entirety of resources (modules, sensors, etc.) and possible combinations is called *perception graph*. Such graph can be used to visualize all possible chain combinations for different perception tasks.

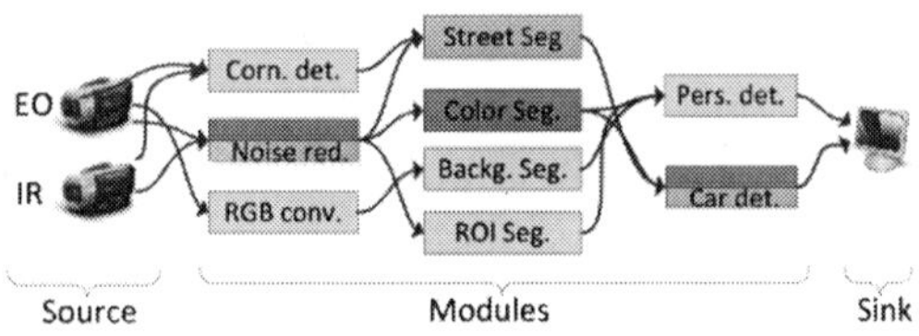

Figure 2. Perception graph. Interaction between sources, perception modules and possible chaining.

Figure 2. illustrates the relationship between sensors, the perception- modules, chains and graph. The graph is represented by the infrared (IR) / electro-optical (EO) sensor, all rectangles, each one providing a different low level capability, and their connections. Furthermore, there are two different perception chains in the figure to detect, e.g., a car from on-board the aircraft, sharing the first and last module (blue and orange rectangles). Both chains can use either an electro-optical sensor or an infrared sensor.

Packaging image processing algorithms into perception modules allow the interpretation of algorithms as capabilities. It also supports reusability and therefore limits the power consumption and processing power onboard UAVs. Figure 2. shows several approaches to achieve the same goal (e.g., detecting a vehicle). A goal oriented usage of perception chains is enabled through detailed descriptions of the modules containing:

- What is the output of a module (*Capabilities*)
- How can a module be combined in a meaningful way (*Requirements*)
- Under which circumstances can a module be used (*Constraints*)

Furthermore, there is a need for a managing entity that loads and interprets the module descriptions to create relational knowledge. Such knowledge is used to identify the availability of low level and high level capabilities depending on given circumstances. The statements also provide information about possible module combinations to create perception chains that provide high level capabilities (HLCs). These high level capabilities in turn can be used to achieve different perception tasks.

In this paper we therefore propose an ontology based approach, using the knowledge representation language OWL, that has been first introduced in [1], to create a knowledge database. This knowledgebase can be inferred by a reasoning mechanism to create statements, describing which resources are available and how they can be used.

This paper is structured as follows: The structure and concept of the presented ontology is being explained in section 2. In section 2.A the class taxonomy is being presented. Next, in section 2.B we will describe the differences between persistent and dynamic individuals. In section 2.C we get into detail with the *resource-capability-resource* concept. The data and object properties are discussed in section 2.D. In the last part of section 2 we describe the rules of the Semantic Web Rules Language (SWRL). In section 3 the experimental evaluation and results are being presented. First, in section 3.A we show how we realize the identification of available high level capabilities. Next, in section 3.B methods to provide valid perception chains are being exposed. In section 3.C we discuss the results for a proof-of-concept ontology. In section 4 there is a conclusion and an outlook into future work.

II. STRUCTURE AND CONCEPT OF THE ONTOLOGY

The ontology has been created using the Web Ontology Language OWL [6]. Three versions of OWL are available:

- OWL Lite, very inexpressive and mostly used just to create taxonomies
- OWL DL (description logic), suitable for practical applications
- OWL Full, too expressive creating situations, where the inference mechanism will loop infinitely (see [6] for details).

Since OWL DL is widespread and has an advanced tool and library support it is used to model the presented ontology. OWL contains three main concepts to model information: classes (concepts), individuals (instances) and properties (roles).

A. *Class Taxonomy*

The OWL classes serve as group container for different types of individuals (In OWL individuals are instances of (real) objects that belong to special class, e.g., "Sony CBR" is an individual of the class "Sensor"). There are two ways how an individual can be assigned to a class:

1. When an individual is loaded into the ontology it gets its main class (e.g., an electro optical sensor would belong to the class "EOSensor" (Figure 3.)).
2. The individual gets additional class assignments by the inference mechanism.

Our ontology has six top level classes:

Concept: contains the definition of the high and low level capabilities. Low level capabilities (LLC) are split into more detailed groups, for example sensor-, image processing- and platform capabilities. LLCs are provided by resources like perception modules or sensors. Simultaneously, each module needs a predefined set of LLCs as input so it can work as intended. The input LLC required by a module though is different to the LLC that is provided by this module. High level capabilities are used by perception tasks, which can be commanded from a third party system. The more detailed subdivision is based on the taxonomy presented in [7].

Environment: covers all individuals to describe the composition of the ground, daytime, weather and lighting conditions (e.g., sky formations).

Hardware: describes the sensors and sensor mountings that are attached to the Unmanned Aerial Vehicle or another platform. Subdivision categories of the sensor class are radar, thermal, optical, laser and virtual sensor.

Platform: includes the classes that describe the user of the S&PMS. The subcategories are aerial platform, ground platform and human team.

Software: implies the image processing algorithms represented as perception modules and other services (e.g., a geo information service (GIS Service)).

Status: This class is empty when the S&PMS is started. It states if any individual is available and can be used or not. The inference mechanism assigns each individual to its status class. E.g., if a module can provide a certain low level capability the module is assigned to the "operative module" class and the capability that is provided by this module to the "available low level capability" class.

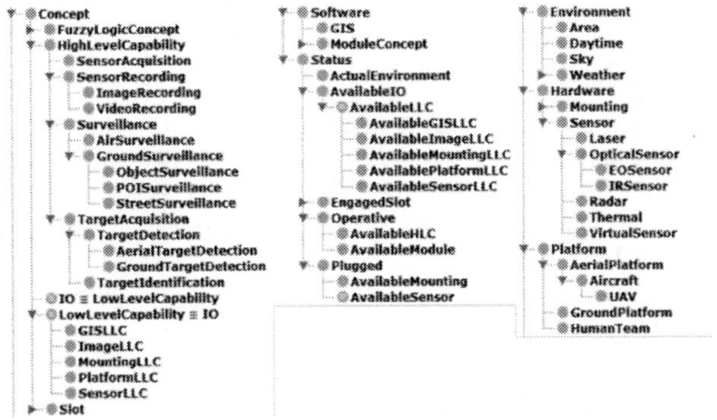

Figure 3. Taxonomy of the ontology.

Figure 3. illustrates the taxonomy of the ontology. In total there are 123 classes.

B. *Persistent and dynamic individuals*

The concept of the ontology takes two different behaviors of individuals into account: the *persistent individuals* are always a part of the ontology and *dynamic loaded individuals*, based on the connected systems. The ontology itself contains only high and low level capabilities and their assigned SWRL Rules (see section E.). These capabilities are modelled by an expert and remain persistent in the database. When the S&PMS is loaded or services and sensors are connected to the S&PMS, the represented individuals (e.g. *Sony Sensor1*) are loaded into the ontology. If a sensor stops working or a perception module crashes, the representative individual is removed from the ontology. As soon as the system notices a change in the ontology the "reasoner" gets invoked to update the overall status of the ontology and notify the S&PMS about system changes. Depending on services and sensors connected, and with respect to requirements and constraints of perception modules that are modelled using SWRL Rules, different low and high level capabilities, sensors and modules are unlocked. The reasoner infers, using SWRL rules and OWL axioms, which individuals can be assigned to the status classes mentioned before in section A.

C. *The resource-capability-resource concept*

Since there are individuals that are added and removed from the ontology in a frequent way during runtime, it is not possible to make a statement about available individuals. For this reason you can never tell, which resources (e.g., modules, sensors, etc.) are currently available hence it is not possible to connect two individuals directly. Therefore we introduced the resource-capability-resource concept with permanent capability individuals that are always a part of the ontology and therefore can be used as a reference to create rules for individuals that are dynamically added to the ontology. These permanent low level capability individuals can be seen as input and output configurations for image processing modules or other resources.

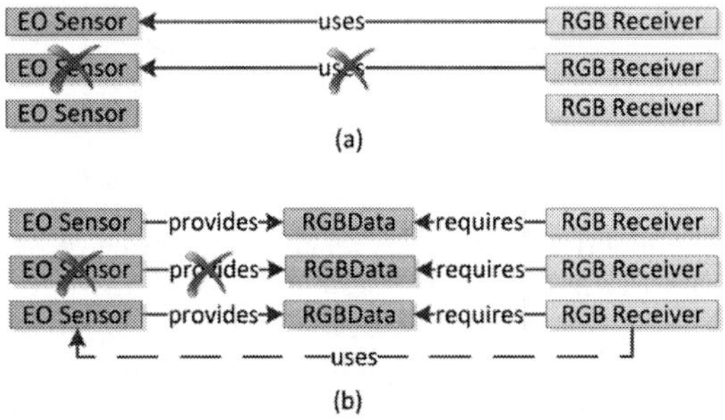

Figure 4. Resource-capability-resource vs. resource-resource connection.

Figure 4. illustrates the difference between the direct connection of resources and the usage of capability individuals between two resources. In (a) the sensor and module are connected directly. Removing the targeted sensor (*EO Sensor*) implies removing the rule from the source module (*RGB Receiver*), because there is no more reference to the target. Re-adding the targeted sensor does however not imply adding the rule to the source module since the source module does not get notified about the existence of the targeted sensor. Another reason against solution (a) is the fact that during modelling time of e.g., *RGB Receiver* there is no knowledge about other resources like sensors or modules. So it would not be possible to create a rule that connects both resources since there is no way to get the information of the existence of e.g., *EO Sensor*.

In (b) each resource holds rules connected to a capability-individual. In this case, when *EO Sensor* gets deleted, only rules included in *EO Sensor* get removed and no other resource is "touched". When *EO Sensor* gets added again, its rules get added too. Since the individual *RGBData* is a permanent individual that is always a part of the ontology, rules that are used by *RGB Receiver* can reference it. Using the inference mechanism a "*uses*" relationship between the sensor and the module can be established.

D. *Data and Object properties*

In OWL we see two different property types, the object and the data properties. Data properties are used to connect individuals with their data represented as parameters. These parameters can be of different built-in types, e.g., string, integer, byte, date or bool. In our ontology, data properties are used to describe the parameters of an image processing algorithm and other numeric information.

Object properties are used to describe relationships between individuals. The most common property is the "is-a" relation between classes (e.g., UAV *is-a* Aircraft). Each object property has several characteristics that can be assigned to it to affect its functional role (e.g., functional, transitive, reflexive, etc.). Additional information can be found in [8]. Within the framework there are four main object properties and their inverses (TABLE I.).

TABLE I. OBJECT PROPERTIES: LEFT: PROPERTY, RIGHT: INVERSE PROPERTY.

object properties	
providesCapability	capabilityProvidedBy
requiresCapability	capabilityRequiredBy
uses	usedBy
subCapabilityOf	superCapabilityOf

The first two describe the relationship between a module and its capabilities. The third and fourth describe the relationship between modules and the relationship within capabilities. The "*is-a*"-property to connect individuals with its classes or classes with subclasses is not listed, because it is not a custom property but a basic property that is available in every ontology.

Figure 5. illustrates a usage of the different object properties to describe the relationship between the individuals and their classes. For clarity the inverse properties are omitted.

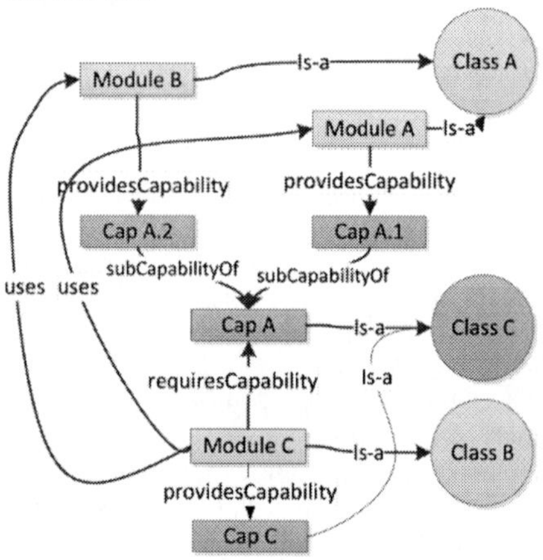

Figure 5. Example for the usage of the different object properties.

E. SWRL Rules

To grant OWL more flexibility and expressive strength it is possible to use rule based languages in combination with the rule markup language (RuleML). Semantic Web Rule Language (SWRL) [9] can be seen as a combination of OWL DL and RuleML. A rule in SWRL is defined as follows:

$$a_1 \wedge a_2 \wedge \dots \wedge a_n \rightarrow b_1 \wedge b_2 \wedge \dots \wedge b_n \quad (1)$$

Variables are called atoms. While a_i describes a precondition (body), b_i describes a post condition (head). Atoms can be class expressions ($C(x)$) or property expressions ($P(x, y)$), in other words relationships between two individuals. There are built in expressions that can be used to model a rule. Some of them are $sameAs(x, y)$, $differentFrom(x, y)$ and $builtin(r, z_1 \dots z_n)$. Built in expressions contain but are not limited to: date, mathematical, string operation. A rule can be read as:

"If precondition X is true, then the post condition is also true."

An empty precondition is always true, an empty post condition always false. All rules that can be accomplish with the OWL axioms can also be modelled with SWRL rules, on the other side there are SWRL rules that cannot be accomplish with OWL axioms.

Each individual that is added dynamically by a service into the ontology contains its own SWRL rule set. Since the capabilities-individuals of the ontology are permanently stored in the database immutable, the SWRL Rules can refer to the individual's names of the capabilities but not to the names of other individuals like sensors or modules.

The SWRL rule belonging to Module C of Figure 5. can be written as follows:

AvailableLLC(Cap A) ^ capabilityProvidedBy(Cap A, ?a)
→ AvailableModule(Module C) ^ (2)
uses(Module C, ?a) ^ providesCapability(Module C, Cap C)

In SWRL "?x" is being used to declare variables. The rule reads as:

"If the individual Cap A belongs to the class AvailableLLC and the individual Cap A has the object property capProvidedBy, referencing to any other individual ?a then assign Module C to the class AvailableModule and assign the object property uses referencing to any other individual ?a to the Module C and the object property providesCap Cap C."

Since there are two other modules that provide Cap A, Module C will belong to the classes "Module" and "AvailableModule" and will have the object property "uses Module B" and "uses Module A" and also have the object property "providesCap Cap C". If another module or a perception task intends to use "Cap C", there are two perception chains that can be used:

- Module B → Module C
- Module A → Module C

III. EXPERIMENTAL EVALUATION

The evaluation of the ontology comprises two categories. It is necessary to know (see section III.A) if at least one perception chain exists, that can solve a given perception task or respectively can provide a high level capability. Next it is necessary to (see section III.B) investigate if all available perception chains for a given HLC are valid and if all possible solutions have been found. Therefore some proof of concept experiments have been done to validate that the identification of HLCs and the perception chains work as expected.

A. *Identifying available high level capabilities*

Testing to check if the ontology identifies available HLCs correctly, can be accomplished directly in the widely used ontology editor Protegé [10]. As mentioned in Figure 3. there is a special class category "Status", more accurate "AvailableHLC" where an HLC individual gets assigned by the reasoner when there is a perception chain that provides this individual. This evaluation includes several SWRL rules for chain components that have to be tested. Each chain component should work self-contained and in combination with other components. Each component requires a *positive* and a *negative* test. The positive test describes a situation where the configuration of the ontology provides individuals that should allow the reasoner to assign a given HLC to the "AvailableHLC" class. For the negative test, the ontology gets changed in a way, that there is no valid path anymore to assign the HLC to the "AvailableHLC" class.

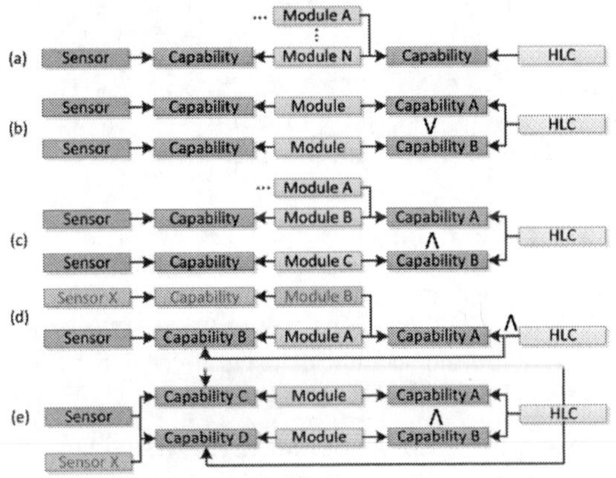

Figure 6. Five chain components that can appear during modelling perception chains.

Figure 6. illustrates five different chain components that can appear in the modelling phase of HLCs. For each component there are different SWRL rules to achieve a desired behavior. The illustration shows a very simple setup starting with the sensor, using one layer of perception modules and connecting it with the HLCs.

(a) is the most simple component where the HLC does need only one capability. The HLC does not care, which or how many modules there are, providing this capability, as long as there is at least one module available. The rule looks like:

AvailableLLC(Capability) ^ capProvidedBy(Capability, ?a) → AvailableModule(HLC) ^ uses(HLC, ?a) (3)

(b) illustrates a component where the HLC can be activated either by "Capability A" or "Capability B". The rule is similar to listing (3) but in this case there is the need for two SWRL Rules, one for "CapabilityA" and the other for "CapabilityB":

AvailableLLC(Capability A) ^ capProvidedBy(Capability A, ?a) → AvailableModule(HLC) ^ uses(HLC, ?a)

(4)

AvailableLLC(Capability B) ^ capProvidedBy(Capability B, ?a) → AvailableModule(HLC) ^ uses(HLC, ?a)

In (c) there is an "and"-relationship between "CapabilityA" and "CapabilityB". The HLC does need both capabilities to get classified as "AvailableHLC". In Figure 6. there are two possible configurations: (Module A ∧ Module C) and (Module B ∧ Module C). The corresponding rule is:

AvailableLLC(Capability A) ^ AvailableLLC(Capability B) ^ capProvidedBy(Capability A, ?a) ^ capProvidedBy (Capability B, ?b) → AvailableModule(HLC) ^ uses(HLC, ?a) ^ uses(HLC, ?b) (5)

(d) shows a more restrictive component. Here it is not enough that there is a perception module that provides "Capability A"; there is also the restriction that the module that provides "Capability A" should also use "Capability B". This guarantees that only the combination (Sensor ∧ Module A) but not the combination (Sensor X ∧ Module B) is a valid chain.

AvailableLLC(Capability A) ^ AvailableLLC(Capability B) ^ capProvidedBy(Capability A, ?a) ^ capProvidedBy (Capability B, ?b)^ uses(?a, ?b) → AvailableModule(HLC) ^ uses(HLC, ?a) (6)

The rule in listing (6) looks similar to listing (5), expect that in (6) there is a "*uses(?a,?b)*" in the body that determines that individual "?a" that also provides "Capability A" has to use individual "?b", which also provides "Capability B".

(e) illustrates a exception where the HLC does need both capabilities "Capability A" and "Capability B". But in this case it must be guaranteed that data, which is used by the modules providing both capabilities, must be from the same sensor.

AvailableLLC(Capability A) ^ AvailableLLC(Capability B) ^ AvailableLLC(Capability C) ^ AvailableLLC(Capability D) ^ capProvidedBy(Capability A, ?a) ^ capProvidedBy(Capability B, ?b) ^ capProvidedBy(Capability C, ?d) ^ capProvidedBy(Capability D, ?e) ^ uses(?a, ?c) ^ uses(?b, ?c) → AvailableModule(HLC) ^ uses(HLC, ?a) ^ uses(HLC, ?b) (7)

To realize the behavior shown in (e) it is necessary to introduce another variable "?c" representing an individual. This individual has to be used by both modules, the ones that provide "Capability A" and the others that provide "Capability B". If "Capability C" would be provided only by "Sensor" and "Capability D" would be provided only by "Sensor X" all capability and perception module individuals would be available but the HLC would still be not available because the rule "*uses(?a,?c) ^ uses(?b,?c)*" from listing (7) would be false.

B. Provide valid perception chains

After collecting information about available high level capabilities it is necessary to verify that the provided combinations of perception modules (in form of perception chains) result in the correct outcome. The list of existing perception chains for a specific HLC does not allow chains that cannot handle the perception task. Therefore the chain count as well as the chain composition is tested against an expert model. All valid chains must be represented. The concatenation and validation of modules into perception chains is done outside the ontology in a special application that can read, write and parse the ontology. The algorithm checks the dependency from one individual to another, starting with the HLC individuals. Recursively each dependency is put into a list (the perception chain list). If an individual has more than one dependency, the chain gets split. The process ends, when an individual has no more dependencies to other individuals. Individual can have multiple SWRL rules, resulting in equal chains. During the concatenation process chains can arise that are formally correct but not valid for the specific HLC since not all low level capabilities can be satisfied within the chain. After the recursive process terminates, duplicates and invalid chains are filtered. There are some cases where the algorithm cannot filter all invalid chains due to rule complexity. In these cases, special data properties are parsed after the initial validation. Whichever parameters are set, special filtering mechanisms are being triggered inside the application to erase the remaining invalid chains.

To guarantee that all valid chains have been found smaller ontologies can be manually matched against an expert design result. For bigger ontologies the complexity rises with each individual added. Above a certain ontology size it gets very difficult for an expert to observe all possible outcomes. It may also be the case that the inference mechanism discovers perception chains, which the expert did not intend to create. This outcome must also be checked against an expert's design results manually. This can be an advantage since solution can arise that are more intelligent or less resource intensive. But it can also be a disadvantage due to the difficult way to evaluate the systems correct way of working.

C. Proof of concept

Based on the founding functions in A) and B) a more general proof of concept was conducted using the example depicted in Figure 6. . The perception graph obtained from the ontology is illustrated in Figure 7.

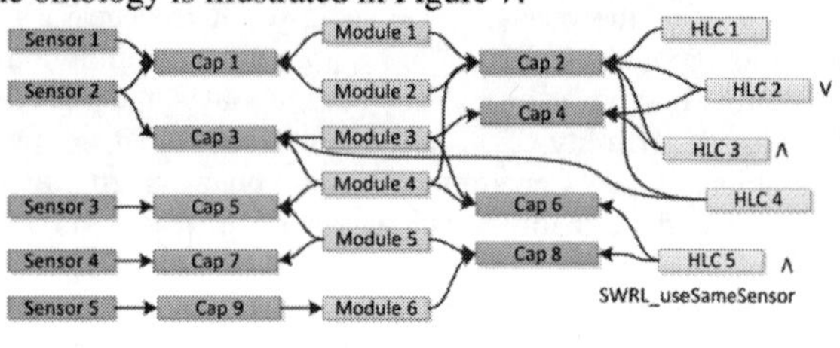

Figure 7. Perception graph generated by example ontology

The system assumes all resources (sensors and modules) to be available and operational. From this point all available HLCs and their perception chains are calculated. Starting the reasoner, we can observe that all HLCs are available like expected (see TABLE II. (a)).

Next each sensor is deactivated until no HLC is available. Each step the perception chains are recalculated by the inference mechanism. The results can be observed in TABLE II. One can see that the modeled rules are working as anticipated: the available HLCs and chain count decreases.

TABLE II. EVALUATING THE DEACTIVATION OF SENSORS

Sensor	Module	HLC	Chains
Sensor 1	Module 1	HLC 1	6
Sensor 2	Module 2	HLC 2	7
Sensor 3	Module 3	HLC 3	6
Sensor 4	Module 4	HLC 4	3
Sensor5	Module 5	HLC 5	1
	Module 6		

(a)

Sensor	Module	HLC	Chains
Sensor 1	Module 1	HLC 1	4
Sensor 2	Module 2	HLC 2	5
Sensor 3	Module 3	HLC 3	4
Sensor 4	Module 4	HLC 4	3
Sensor5	Module 5	HLC 5	1
	Module 6		

(b)

Sensor	Module	HLC	Chains
Sensor 1	Module 1	HLC 1	1
Sensor 2	Module 2	HLC 2	1
Sensor 3	Module 3	HLC 3	0
Sensor 4	Module 4	HLC 4	0
Sensor5	Module 5	HLC 5	1
	Module 6		

(c)

Sensor	Module	HLC	Chains
Sensor 1	Module 1	HLC 1	0
Sensor 2	Module 2	HLC 2	0
Sensor 3	Module 3	HLC 3	0
Sensor 4	Module 4	HLC 4	0
Sensor5	Module 5	HLC 5	0
	Module 6		

(d)

In TABLE II (a) all sensors are available hence all modules and HLCs are available with a different amount of perception chains. In TABLE II (b) "Sensor 1" is deactivated. Since "Sensor 1" and "Sensor 2" provide the same capability no module is being affected but the chain count for "HLC1"-"HLC3" decreases.

TABLE III. CHAIN COMPOSITIONS FOR (A) FROM TABLE II

HLC 1	6
Sensor 1	Module 1
Sensor 1	Module 2
Sensor 2	Module 1
Sensor 2	Module 2
Sensor 2	Module 4
Sensor 3	Module 4

HLC 2	7
Sensor 1	Module 1
Sensor 1	Module 2
Sensor 2	Module 1
Sensor 2	Module 2
Sensor 2	Module 4
Sensor 3	Module 4
Sensor 2	Module 3

HLC 3	6	
Sensor 1	Module 1	Module 3
Sensor 1	Module 2	Module 3
Sensor 2	Module 1	Module 3
Sensor 2	Module 2	Module 3
Sensor 2	Module 4	Module 3
Sensor 3	Module 4	Module 3

HLC 4	3
Sensor 2	Module 1
Sensor 2	Module 2
Sensor 2	Module 4

HLC 5	1	
Sensor 3	Module 4	Module 5

TABLE IV. CHAIN COMPOSITIONS FOR (B) FROM TABLE II

HLC 1	4
Sensor 2	Module 1
Sensor 2	Module 2
Sensor 2	Module 4
Sensor 3	Module 4

HLC 2	5
Sensor 2	Module 1
Sensor 2	Module 2
Sensor 2	Module 4
Sensor 3	Module 4
Sensor 2	Module 3

HLC 3	4	
Sensor 2	Module 1	Module 3
Sensor 2	Module 2	Module 3
Sensor 2	Module 4	Module 3
Sensor 3	Module 4	Module 3

HLC 4	3
Sensor 2	Module 1
Sensor 2	Module 2
Sensor 2	Module 4

HLC 5	1	
Sensor 3	Module 4	Module 5

TABLE V. CHAIN COMPOSITIONS FOR (C) FROM TABLE II

HLC	Count	Chain		
HLC 1	1	Sensor 3	Module 4	
HLC 2	1	Sensor 3	Module 4	
HLC 3	0			
HLC 4	0			
HLC 5	1	Sensor 3	Module 4	Module 5

When deactivating "Sensor2" (cf. (c)) three modules are not operative any more since there is no sensor that can provide the required data respectively capabilities. As a hoped consequence "HLC3" and "HLC 4" is being deactivated and the chain count for the operative HLCs drops drastically. When "Sensor 3" is also being deactivated we can observer that in (d) "Module 4" stops working and there are no more available high level capabilities.

TABLE III. TABLE IV. and TABLE V. list the possible module compositions for the results illustrated in TABLE II. (a), (b) and (c). In TABLE IV. one can see that no more chain compositions for *Sensor 1* are available anymore. In TABLE V. only chain compositions using *Sensor 3* are available since *Sensor 1* and *Sensor 2* are deactivated and for the other two sensors there are no perception chains. Overall the experiments show a supposed behavior of the inferred results taking the modeled relationship and SWRL rules into account. The results prove a suitable usage of the ontology to model sensor and data processing resources using OWL.

IV. CONCLUSION AND FUTURE WORK

We presented an approach to manage sensor and data resources with an ontology based knowledge management system. It was shown how the knowledge representing language OWL can be used respectively. The presented solution proposes to model image processing algorithms as perception modules providing different low level capabilities, which in turn can be combined to high level capabilities, representing various perception tasks e.g., vehicle detection. For each task different perception chains are calculated, dependent on the current environmental situation and platform setup respectively resource configuration (sensors, algorithms, etc.).

An important next step is to develop a decision-making system that takes available perception chains for a given perception task in account and determines, based on different parameters and meta-information, which chain is most suitable to solve the given task.

The system shall be further tested in a multi UAV scenario where each UAV has a different sensor and perception module configuration. The aim here is to combine different capabilities onboard UAVs and let the UAVs collaborate to solve a complex perception task as a team.

Eventually investigations are planned in human-machine scenario, where a helicopter operator can fall back to S&PMS functions that assist him during his mission and therefore reduce the operator's workload. The operator can choose between different automation levels so that the S&PMS can process full perception tasks or only parts of it [11]. In this scenario, the human capabilities are a part of the knowledge base and are modeled into the ontology. The inference mechanism takes the human capabilities into account when generating perception chains for different perception tasks. For example, when there is no algorithmic way for a processing step, the S&PMS can make use of human capability to still find an adequate perception chain.

REFERENCES

[1] D. Smirnov and P. Stuetz, "Knowledge elicitation and representation for module based perceptual capabilities onboard UAVs," in *AIAA SciTech 2014*, 2014.

[2] C. Hellert, D. Smirnov, M. Russ, and P. Stuetz, "A High Level Active Percpetion Concept For UAV Mission Scenarios," in *Deutscher Luft- und Raumfahrtkongress 2012*, pp. 1–9, 2012.

[3] C. Hellert, D. Smirnov, and P. Stuetz, "Ontologiedesign für Sensor- und Perzeptionsfähigkeiten von UAVs," in *Deutscher Luft- und Raumfahrtkongress 2014*, 2014.

[4] M. Russ and P. Stütz, "Airborne sensor and perception management: A conceptual approach for surveillance UAS," in *Proceedings of the 15th International Conference on Information Fusion (FUSION2012)*, pp. 2444–2451, 2012.

[5] M. Russ and P. Stuetz, "Application of a probabilistic market-based approach in UAV sensor & perception management," in *Information Fusion (FUSION), 2013 16th International Conference on*, pp. 676–683, 2013.

[6] W3C OWL Working Group, "OWL 2 Web Ontology Language Document Overview," 2013. [Online]. Available: http://www.w3.org/TR/owl2 overview/. [Accessed: 08 May 2013].

[7] M. Gomez et al., "An ontology-centric approach to sensor-mission assignment," *Knowl. Eng. Pract. Patterns*, pp. 347–363, 2008.

[8] M. Horridge et al., "A Practical Guide To Building OWL Ontologies Using Protégé 4 and CO-ODE Tools," Manchester, 2011.

[9] I. Horrocks, P. F. Patel-schneider, H. Boley, S. Tabet, B. Grosof, and M. Dean, "SWRL : A Semantic Web Rule Language Combining OWL and RuleML," *W3C Memb. Submiss. 21*, no. May 2004, pp. 1–20, 2004.

[10] "Protégé project." [Online]. Available: http://protege.stanford.edu.

[11] C. Ruf and P. Stütz, "Model-driven Sensor Operation Assistance for a Transport Helicopter Crew in Manned-Unmanned Teaming Missions : Selecting the Automation Level by Machine Decision-making," in *7th International Conference on Applied Human Factors and Ergonomics (AHFE2016)*, 2016.

Selecting Adequate Aerial Perceptual Functions with Fuzzy Logic

Christian Hellert and Peter Stütz
Institute of Flight Systems
University of the Bundeswehr Munich
Neubiberg, Germany
e-mail: [christian.hellert,peter.stuetz]@unibw.de

Abstract—**The increasing interest in higher automation of unmanned aerial vehicles (UAV) rises the challenge of implementing sophisticated perception functions. Since such functions, whether being used for navigational (e.g., sense & avoid) or surveillance purposes (e.g., object detection & tracking), are heavily influenced by environmental conditions. Hence, a careful selection and parametrization of the perception functions during flight is required to maintain perceptual efficiency on-board the UAV. This paper introduces a method to predict the performance of perception functions, allowing a ranking for algorithm selection. The proposed method uses expert knowledge to model the influence of the environment on the perception functions using fuzzy logic. An evaluation of the proposed method is performed with an aerial vehicle detection algorithm on an imagery dataset, generated from virtual simulation, taking into account fog density and cloud cover. The results show that the method can predict the algorithms performance in general and has the advantage of expressive modelling of the expert knowledge.**

Keywords-Perception functions; fuzzy logic; algorithm selection; algorithm ranking; expert knowledge.

I. INTRODUCTION

The automation of unmanned aerial vehicle (UAV) navigation and guidance is an active research area. Further, the on-board analysis of mission sensor data is needed for environmental awareness and reconnaissance and surveillance missions. The anticipated benefit of higher levels of automation of UAVs is seen by reducing costs, being able to control multiple UAVs by a single operator, and deploying UAVs in areas where no infrastructure for communication and navigation is available.

Mature data processing algorithms for UAV mission sensors are designed for specific use cases, for example often in the domain of object detection and tracking. Therefore, the algorithms regularly produce reliable results only under certain constraints. However, during UAV missions, the environment can change considerable for example in terms of ground surfaces, field of view, lighting conditions and atmospheric effects, influencing the sensor data quality, as well as the performance of data processing algorithms. Hence, a management of sensors and sensor data processing algorithms is advisable to assure the quality of the automated sensor data evaluation in the aforementioned application domains.

For this purpose, a respective system concept was introduced in [1], namely the Sensor & Perception Management System (SPMS). Thereby, the SPMS selects appropriate sensor types, e.g., electro-optical (EO), infrared (IR), and light detection and ranging (LIDAR), and applies adequate sensor data processing algorithms to accomplish certain perception tasks, such as object detection, tracking, and obstacle recognition. Selecting and parametrizing perceptual capabilities according to the current environmental situation eventually results in maintaining algorithm performance.

We developed a method to predict the quality or performance of such perceptual capabilities of the SPMS, allowing the ranking and selection of the best suited algorithms. In Section II, the related work is briefly shown and Section III presents an algorithm selection method using a weighting function based on fuzzy logic and compares its performance prediction for a selected vehicle detection algorithm with ground-truth obtained from an evaluation dataset. The results of our method are presented and discussed in Section IV. Section V closes the paper with a conclusion and future work.

II. RELATED WORK

Rice [2] formulated a general concept for the problem of selecting an algorithm from a set of algorithms. Using a case base, which contains cases from learning or observing successful executed tasks with their solution, is as a general methodology for algorithm selection and was proposed by [3]. A similarity measurement [4] compares the new task with the case base using the tasks problem description to select the appropriate solution.

Hochgeschwender et al. [5] addressed the problem of selecting marker detection algorithms, based on image interest point detection, under different illuminations in an indoor scenario to maximize detection performance. During a training phase, the performance of the algorithms is evaluated and image histograms, as well as respective algorithm parameters, are stored whenever the performance seems reasonable. The selection algorithm uses the Kullback-Leibler divergence as measurement to compare the current image histogram with the saved ones to rank the algorithms.

An automatic selection approach for color constancy algorithms is proposed in [6]. They extract simple features from images and using a Mamdani-type fuzzy inference system to reason about the appropriate algorithm. Thereby, the fuzzy rules and sets are learned from example.

In [7], an approach for selecting sensor processing algorithms with Bayesian networks is proposed. Here, the environmental and sensor requirements of the algorithms, as well as their implementation quality, is modelled to estimate the performance of the algorithms.

A meta-learning approach is used by [8][9] for ranking the algorithms with a relative score, in respect of the algorithm with the highest score. They extract meta-features (e.g., mean illumination or noise-signal ratio of an imagery dataset) and evaluate the performance of the algorithms from the learning datasets. Afterwards, a meta-learner uses the performance and meta-features to derive a model, enabling the computing of relative performances of the algorithms on a new dataset. This method allows the automatic learning of an algorithm selection mechanism without the need for explicit expert knowledge as required in the here presented method. However, a sophisticated learning dataset must be provided to achieve reliable results.

Other approaches [10]–[12] also model the algorithms constraints with expert knowledge and apply machine inferencing about the availability of the algorithms [13]. Our approach now uses the idea of modelling the environmental impact with probabilities [7], since they can be considered as not completely observable. It is realized with fuzzy logic where expert knowledge is mapped to fuzzy rules. The notation and concept introduced by [2] is used in this paper.

III. METHOD

The selection of an algorithm requires a ranking metric. In the proposed method, a weighting function predicts the performance of the algorithm with respect to a given perceptive task (e.g., vehicle detection), in dependency of a feature vector describing the actual environment state. The weighting function returns a normalized value, describing how successful a certain algorithm can be applied. Fig. 1 shows an overview of the proposed algorithm selection method. The selection function takes the algorithm set and the environment state vector to choose an algorithm with a parameter set, in dependency of the calculated performance. Expert knowledge declare the impact of the environment state vector on the algorithms performance.

The algorithm selection s requires features f_x to compute the performance of the algorithms in a set A, where each algorithm $a_i \in A$ has parameter sets $p_j \in a_i$. The following formula expresses the algorithm selection function:

$$a_i(p_j) = s(f_x, A) \quad (1)$$

with x denoting a candidate from the problem space and $f_x = \{x_0, \ldots, x_{K-1}\}$ the extracted features. K is the number of feature elements. The weighting function w computes the

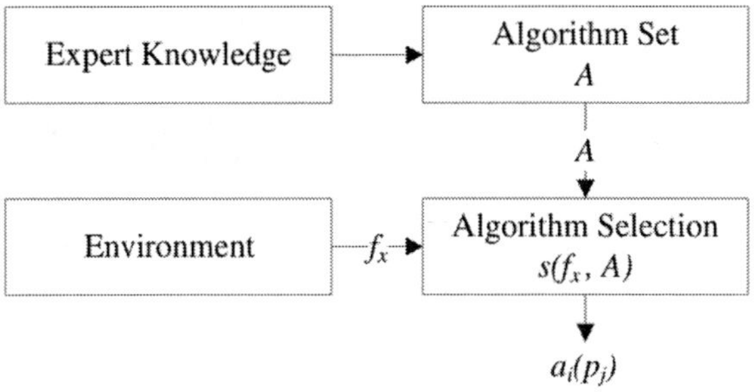

Figure 1. Algorithm selection method using expert knowledge to predict the algorithms performance.

predicted performance for one specific algorithm within one specific parameter set. The maximum performance of an algorithm a_i considering its parameter sets results from

$$\max_{p \in a_i} \left(w\left(f_x, a_{i,p}\right) \cdot q\left(a_{i,p}\right) \right) \quad (2)$$

where the variable q states the quality, or general usability, of the algorithm for a given parameter set. For example, the quality of an object detection algorithm can be measured by its average precision.

In [1][14] the concept for sensor and perception management (SPM) was introduced, presenting the idea of having a set of dedicated *perception chains*, each being a combination of several algorithms a_i to fulfill a specific perception task. An example perception chain could consist of a *segmentation stage*, followed by *interest point detection* and eventually a *classification algorithm*. This work is part of such SPM concept and therefore the equation (2) extends to

$$\sum_{a_i \in c_m} \left(\max_{p \in a_i} \left(w\left(f_x, a_{i,p}\right) \cdot q\left(a_{i,p}\right) \right) \right) \frac{1}{N} \quad (3)$$

where $c_m \in C$ is a perception chain containing algorithms a_i from A. $C = \{c_0, \ldots, c_m, \ldots, c_M\}$ comprises all perception chains designed for a perception task and N is the number of algorithms in c_m. The selection function calculates the perception chain performance, using equation (3), and returns the perception chain with the highest performance, including the related parameter sets.

The computation of the algorithms performance within the weighting function requires a method to compute the impact of the feature vector f_x on the algorithm's $a_{i,p}$ performance. A classical assessment of the impact of the feature vector from examples would require a large dataset with aerial imagery, however existing ones [15]–[17] are lacking the necessary environmental variations. As an alternative approach, here, experts assess the impact of

Figure 2. Example images from the dataset: In the first row, the cloud cover increases from the left to right. The illumination decrease slightly and the shadows are more blurred while the cloud cover increases. In the second row, the fog density increases from left to right and the contrast declines.

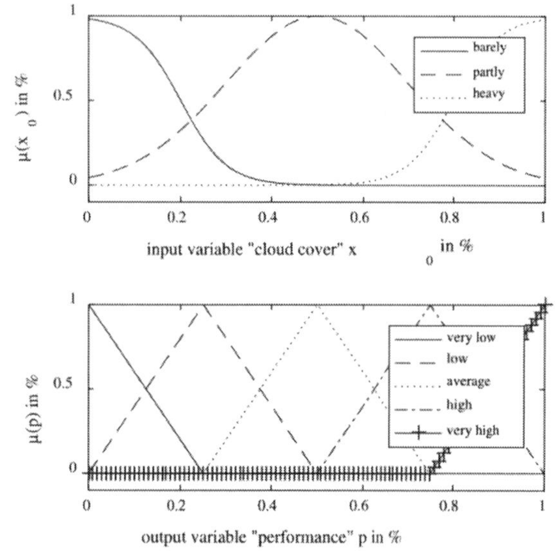

Figure 3. Fuzzy membership functions of cloud cover and performance variable: The y-axis denotes the degree of membership. Note that cloud cover and fog density are modelled equally.

environmental features from their experience and knowledge. Here, the notation of *if-then fuzzy logic rules* were chosen, because it is human understandable and machine-processible. In addition, since the environment is not completely observable, the *if-then fuzzy logic rule* notation is capable of modelling vague knowledge. Such fuzzy inference system requires the *fuzzification* of the input values from the feature vector by membership functions.

In a given toy problem, two input variables were selected for describing ambient environmental features, the *cloud cover* $x_0 \in f_x$ and the *fog density* $x_1 \in f_x$, since they affect illumination, shadow intensity and significance of gradients in images. For illustration, Fig. 2 shows the cloud cover input and the performance output value with their membership functions.

The fuzzy rules activate the related membership function, whereby the input value of x_0, e.g., the cloud cover measurement, determines the membership degree $\mu(x_0)$. For example, the rule "*if cloud cover is heavy then performance is average*" activates the cloud cover membership function "*heavy*", for $x_0 = 0.8$ resulting in $\mu(x_0) = 0.5$. Afterwards, the membership function "*average*" of the output variable performance receives the same degree of membership. A *deffuzification* step computes the center of the area under the "*average*" curve, cut off by the degree of membership line. For multiple input values, the center of the union of the areas is calculated to obtain the performance value. This work uses the Mamdani-type fuzzy inference [18], because of its expressional power which allows a clean modelling of expert knowledge as examined by [19].

IV. Evaluation and Discussion

On the basis of an aerial vehicle detection algorithm, developed by [20], an evaluation of the proposed method is performed. The vehicle detection algorithm uses weak classifiers in a cascade to detect vehicles with Haar-like image features and local binary pattern features. The variables describing the environment are the cloud cover and fog density of the scene as mentioned above. First, the average performance of the algorithm is determined with a ground-truth evaluation dataset obtained in virtual simulation, using Virtual Battlespace 3 (VBS3) [21]. The average performance is then compared with the output of the modelled fuzzy inference system to evaluate the precision of the weighting function.

The dataset includes 22 scenarios from one VBS3 map with fixed cloud cover and fog density values from zero to one, where zero defines clear sky or no fog and one defines full cloud cover or dense fog. Fig. 3 shows some example images form the dataset. Each scenario consists of 7500 images in 1920x1080 resolution with annotations of the vehicle locations. The parameters for the image generation are 50 meter distance from camera to the center of the image and an elevation of -45 degrees. These parameters where selected from the evaluation of the algorithm in [20], where the average performance has the highest score. The image generation process scans the scenarios in a grid with randomly selected azimuth angles and each vehicle from azimuth angles ranging from zero to 360 degrees. The vehicles, 50 per scenario, are randomly placed on the map. The vehicle detection algorithm is tested on each scenario to calculate a receiver operating characteristic (ROC) curve to determine the algorithm's average performance, in dependency of the cloud cover and fog density value separately.

The resulting ROC curves from the scenarios are shown in Fig. 4, where the area under the curve is the measurement for the average performance of the vehicle detection algorithm on the related scenario, and the circles mark the optimal operation point for the classifier. The upper plot in Fig. 4 shows the ROC curves for cloud cover and the one below for influences of the fog density. The scenarios to evaluate the cloud cover impact have zero fog density and the scenarios for evaluating the fog density impact have 50 percent cloud cover.

The fuzzy inference system calculates the prediction of the algorithm performance using as input the cloud cover and fog density and as output the performance. In Fig. 2 the membership functions for the fuzzy variables are shown. The fuzzy rules can be read as follows:

- *If fog density is hardly and cloud cover is barely then performance is high*
- *If fog density is hardly and cloud cover is partly then performance is high*
- *If fog density is hardly and cloud cover is heavy then performance is very high*
- *If fog density is moderate and cloud cover is barely then performance is high*
- *If fog density is dense and cloud cover is barely then performance is average*

With increasing cloud cover, the average performance of the algorithm increases from 62 to 71 percent as depicted in the upper graph of Fig. 5. While the cloud cover increases, the appearance of shadows and the illumination decreases. Therefore, the algorithm is obviously robust against illumination changes and shadows. The error between the calculated performance and the predicted performance is 7.6 percent. In the upper graph of Fig. 5 the error is the highlighted area between performance and prediction curve.

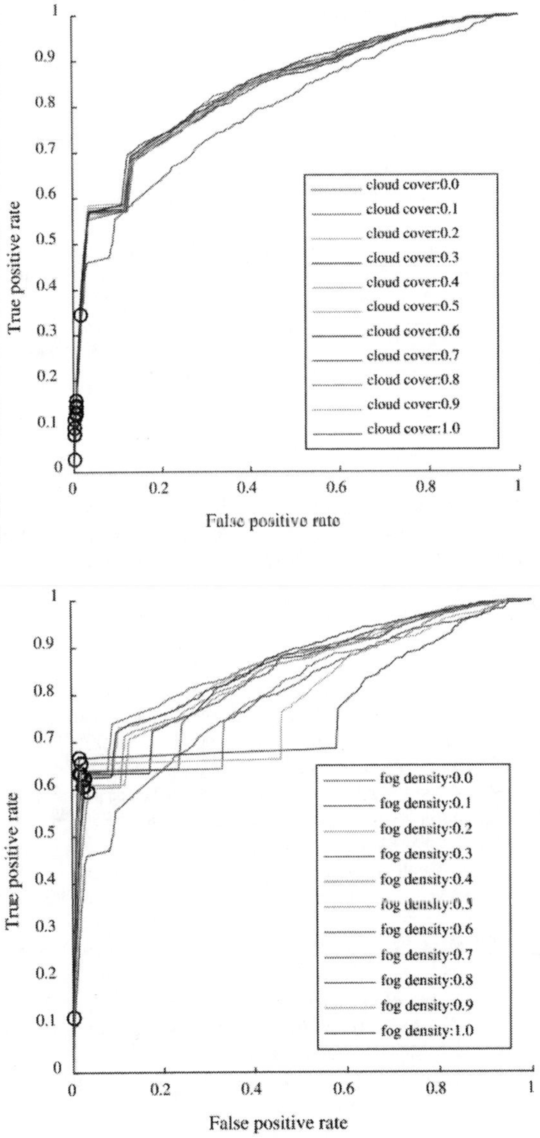

Figure 4. ROC curves of the vehicle detection algorithm for each scenario.

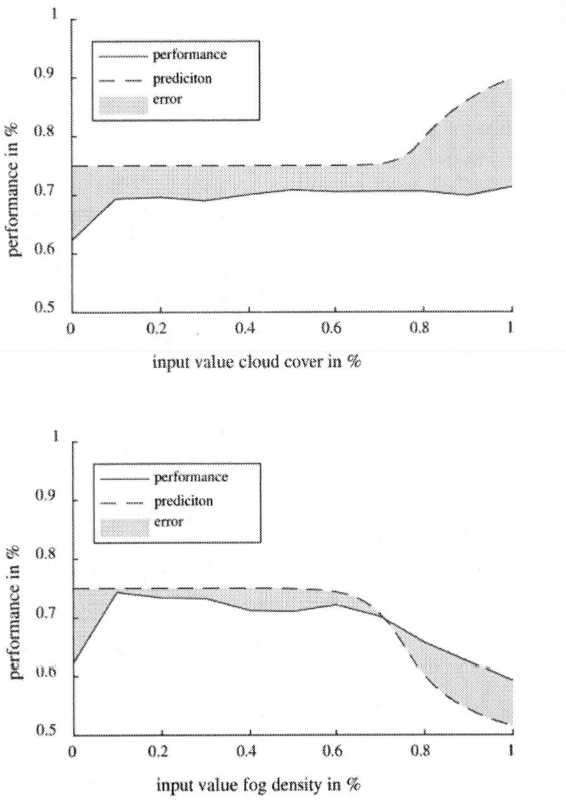

Figure 5. Comparison between evaluated (solid line) and predicted (dashed line) algorithm performance for cloud cover and fog density.

In general, with increasing fog density the average performance decreases, while the image is blurred, reducing the significance of the edges in the image. First, the average performance increases from 62 to 74 percent and then drops to 59 percent. Comparing the calculated performance with the predicted performance results in an error of 0.3 percent (see lower graph of Fig. 5).

It can be observed, that the proposed method can in general describe the trend of environmental impact on the algorithm and is therefore useful for predicting the performance of the algorithm. The advantage of the proposed method is the clear description of the environmental influence, with fuzzy rules from expert knowledge, but the disadvantage is the lack in accuracy between the calculated and predicted performance. The introduction of a greater set of membership functions for the fuzzy variables can increase the accuracy, but it also increases the modelling effort and therefore, detailed expert knowledge is required, but it is unlikely that such detailed knowledge is available. Thus, we recommend a clear set of membership functions.

V. CONCLUSION

The management of perceptual capabilities requires the estimation of the performance of the underlying algorithms in dependency of the environmental state. In this paper, such performance prediction was demonstrated using a fuzzy logic approach. The results show, that it is possible to model the general influence of the environment state at the algorithm performance.

In [6] image features where used to select the best algorithm via learning of an fuzzy inference system. In contrast to our approach, the image data must be available to select the algorithm, while our method can predict the algorithm performance without image data. Tenorth and Beetz [11] use expert knowledge to reason about the appropriate vision algorithm for a personal robot. Unlike our approach, they require detailed expert knowledge. Comparing our method with [5], the modelling of the environmental influences takes less effort, but the performance prediction accuracy is lower. In addition, when expert knowledge is not available, our method cannot be used. Therefore, in a next step, the missing expert knowledge shall be obtained by machine learning approaches to shape the membership function and generate fuzzy rules to enhance the performance prediction accuracy. For future evaluation, a larger scaled dataset will be generated to test learning approaches as well as suitable methods to determine the environmental state vector.

REFERENCES

[1] M. Russ and P. Stütz, "Airborne sensor and perception management: A conceptual approach for surveillance UAS," in *Proceedings of the 15th International Conference on Information Fusion (FUSION2012)*, pp. 2444–2451, 2012.

[2] J. R. Rice, "The Algorithm Selection Problem," *Adv. Comput.*, vol. 15, no. C, pp. 65–118, 1976.

[3] A. Aamodt and E. Plaza, "Case-based reasoning: Foundational issues, methodological variations, and system approaches," *AI Commun.*, vol. 7, no. 1, pp. 39–59, 1994.

[4] P. Cunningham, "A Taxonomy of Similarity Mechanisms for Case-Based Reasoning," *IEEE Trans. Knowl. Data Eng.*, vol. 21, no. 11, pp. 1532–1543, Nov. 2009.

[5] N. Hochgeschwender, M. A. Olivares-Mendez, H. Voos, and G. K. Kraetzschmar, "Context-based selection and execution of robot perception graphs," *IEEE Int. Conf. Emerg. Technol. Fact. Autom. ETFA*, pp. 1–4, 2015.

[6] J. Cepeda-Negrete and R. E. Sanchez-Yanez, "Automatic selection of color constancy algorithms for dark image enhancement by fuzzy rule-based reasoning," *Appl. Soft Comput. J.*, vol. 28, pp. 1–10, 2015.

[7] M. Russ and P. Stuetz, "Application of a probabilistic market-based approach in UAV sensor & perception management," in *Information Fusion (FUSION), 2013 16th International Conference on*, pp. 676–683, 2013.

[8] Q. Sun and B. Pfahringer, "Pairwise meta-rules for better meta-learning-based algorithm ranking," *Mach. Learn.*, vol. 93, no. 1, pp. 141–161, 2013.

[9] K. A. Smith-Miles, "Cross-disciplinary perspectives on meta-learning for algorithm selection," *ACM Comput. Surv.*, vol. 41, no. 1, pp. 1–25, 2008.

[10] G. H. Lim, S. Member, I. H. Suh, S. Member, and H. Suh, "Ontology-Based Unified Robot Knowledge for Service Robots in Indoor Environments," *Syst. Man Cybern. Part A Syst. Humans, IEEE Trans.*, vol. 41, no. 3, pp. 492–509, 2011.

[11] M. Tenorth and M. Beetz, "KnowRob: A knowledge processing infrastructure for cognition-enabled robots," *Int. J. Rob. Res.*, vol. 32, no. 5, pp. 566–590, 2013.

[12] M. Tenorth and M. Beetz, "KnowRob—knowledge processing for autonomous personal robots," *IEEE/RSJ Int. Conf. Intell. Robot. Syst. 2009 (IROS 2009)*, pp. 4261–4266, 2009.

[13] M. Gomez et al., "An ontology-centric approach to sensor-mission assignment," *Knowl. Eng. Pract. Patterns*, pp. 347–363, 2008.

[14] C. Hellert, D. Smirnov, M. Russ, and P. Stuetz, "A High Level Active Perception Concept For UAV Mission Scenarios," in *Deutscher Luft- und Raumfahrtkongress 2012*, 2012.

[15] S. Razakarivony and F. Jurie, "Vehicle detection in aerial imagery : A small target detection benchmark," *J. Vis. Commun. Image Represent.*, vol. 34, pp. 187–203, 2016.

[16] R. Collins, X. Zhou, and S. K. Teh, "An open source tracking testbed and evaluation web site," *IEEE Int. Work. Perform. Eval. Track. Surveill.*, pp. 17–24, 2005.

[17] F. Tanner et al., "Overhead imagery research data set - An annotated data library & tools to aid in the development of computer vision algorithms," *Appl. Imag. Pattern Recognit. Work. (AIPRW), IEEE*, pp. 1–8, 2009.

[18] E. H. Mamdani and S. Assilian, "An experiment in linguistic synthesis with a fuzzy logic controller," *Int. J. Man. Mach. Stud.*, vol. 7, no. 1, pp. 1–13, 1975.

[19] A. Hamam and N. D. Georganas, "A comparison of mamdani and sugeno fuzzy inference systems for evaluating the quality of experience of hapto-audio-visual applications," *HAVE 2008 - IEEE Int. Work. Haptic Audio Vis. Environ. Games Proc.*, no. October, pp. 87–92, 2008.

[20] G. Hummel, D. Smirnov, A. Kronenberg, and P. Stütz, "Prototyping and training of computer vision algorithms in a synthetic UAV mission test bed," in *AIAA SciTech 2014*, pp. 1–10, 2014.

[21] P. Morrison, "White Paper: VBS2 Release Version 2.0," Nelson Bay, Australia, 2012.

Local Edge/Corner Feature Integration for Illumination Invariant Face Recognition

Almabrok Essa and Vijayan Asari

Department of Electrical and Computer Engineering
University of Dayton, Dayton, Ohio, USA
Email: essaa1@udayton.edu, vasari1@udayton.edu

***Abstract*—In this paper, we present a new appearance based feature descriptor, named Local edge/corner Feature Integration (LFI), which efficiently summarizes the local structure of face images. LFI is a nonparametric descriptor that utilizes a combined edge/corner detection strategy. The proposed method uses the approach suggested by Frei and Chen for corner and edge detection with nine different masks. After we obtain the information about corners and edges of the image, for each pixel position, we describe the relationship of pixels to their local neighborhood from the local edge/corner features using the edges and corners information separately. Then, we concatenate these patterns together to form the final LFI feature vector. The performance evaluation of the proposed LFI algorithm is conducted on several publicly available databases and observed promising recognition rates.**

Keywords–Face recognition; Frei-Chen edge detector; modular histogram; chi-square similarity measure; libsvm classifier; local edge/corner feature integration (LFI).

I. INTRODUCTION

During the past few years, face recognition has received a great deal of attention and become one of the most popular research areas in the fields of computer vision, image processing, pattern recognition, and machine learning. The key of each face recognition system is the utilization of the feature extraction technique that must be able to extract features from the face image, which are distinct and stable under different conditions during the image acquisition process.

In the recent years, much research work has been done on extracting image features. Many computer vision applications employ the texture analysis algorithms. Two of the highest performing texture algorithms that based on the concept of local pattern descriptors, namely Local Binary Pattern (LBP) and Local Directional Pattern (LDP), which describe the relationship of pixels to their local neighborhood. They detect only the important local textures by labeling each pixel with the code of texture primitive that best matches the local neighborhood. Fig. 1 shows some of these texture primitives that can be detected by the local pattern descriptors that include spots, line ends, flat area, edges, and corners [1].

LBP is a nonparametric method which extracts local structures of images efficiently by comparing each pixel with its neighboring pixels. If a neighbor pixel has a higher gray value than the center pixel (or the same gray value) then a 1 is assigned to that pixel, which is otherwise a 0. Finally, the LBP binary code for the center pixel is produced by concatenating the eight $1s$ or $0s$, which can be converted to a decimal number to produce the new value of that central pixel. The original LBP operator was introduced by Ojala et al. for texture analysis [2], and has proved a simple yet powerful approach to describe local structures. LBP operator has a number of extensions that have been extensively used in many applications, such as face image analysis [3][4], image and video retrieval [5][6], environment modeling [7][8], visual inspection [9][10], motion analysis [11][12], and biomedical and aerial image analysis [13][14]. LBP-based facial image analysis has been one of the most popular and successful applications in recent years. Nevertheless, LBP considers only first order intensity pattern change in a local neighborhood which fails to extract detailed information especially during changes in face image due to the noise and illumination variation problems.

LDP encodes the directional information in the neighborhood instead of the intensity as LBP does with higher computational cost. LDP is a gray-scale pattern that characterizes the spatial structure of a local image texture. It computes the edge response values in eight different directions at each pixel position by convolving the image with the Kirsch masks in eight different orientations, centered on its own position. Then it uses the relative strength magnitude to encode the image texture. The presence of a corner or an edge shows high response values in some particular directions. Therefore, in order to generate the LDP code, we need to know the n most prominent directions. Then, the top n directional bit responses are set to 1 and the rest $(8-n)$ bits of 8-bit LDP pattern are set to 0 [15][16]. Since the edge responses are more noise and illumination insensitive than intensity values, the resultant LDP feature maintains more information than LBP and describes the local primitives stably, including different types of curves, corners, and junctions. However, LDP technique still suffers in non-monotonic illumination variation and random noise.

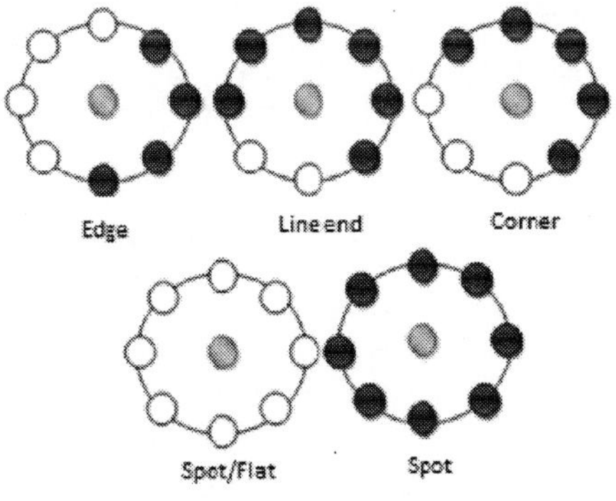

Figure 1. Different texture primitives detected by local pattern descriptors.

In this paper, we present a new local pattern descriptor, named Local edge/corner Feature Integration (LFI) that is simple but effective, and it can be a potential tool to extract image features. LFI is a nonparametric method which extracts local structures of images efficiently by comparing each pixel with its neighboring pixels from edge/corner responses separately, then combining these thresholding responses to form the final code. Unlike LDP whose codes are generated by setting the top n directional bit responses to 1 and the rest to 0, which may ignore some important information in the local neighborhood. LFI uses the information of edge/corner changes around pixels and labels the pixels by thresholding a 3×3 neighboring pixels with the central pixel separately then considering the results as binary codes. After that concatenates these binary codes to form the final LFI feature vector.

The rest of the paper is organized as follows. In Section 2, the mathematical details of the proposed LFI algorithm is provided. Discussion on the datasets and experimental results are presented in Section 3. Finally, the conclusion is drawn in Section 4.

II. Local Edge/Corner Feature Integration (LFI)

This work aims to improve the face recognition accuracy under illumination-variant environments by detecting much stable edges especially in dark areas, which can be done by the help of Frei-Chen edge detector [17]. The proposed LFI technique can be summarized into three stages: edge/corner detection, binary encoding and decoding, and feature integration. Fig. 2 illustrates the framework of the proposed technique. The details of each stage are described below.

A. *Corner/Edge Detection*

We suggest to utilize the properties of Frei-Chen edge detector to extract more detailed corner and edge information from input image. Frei-Chen edge detector works as nine convolution masks that work on a 3×3 window size denoted as K_i for $i = 1, 2, ..., 9$ as shown in Fig. 3. The first four masks K_i for $i = 1, ..., 4$ are used to find the edges' subspace, the first two of them K_1 and K_2 represent the isotropic smoothed gradient weighting function, which will be supported by the second two K_3 and K_4 to span the above edge's subspace by contributing to the magnitude of the edge's subspace components. The second four kernels K_i for $i = 5, ..., 8$ are utilized to find the corners' subspace. By summing all of these four, all possible discrete realizations of the points can be detected. The last one K_9 is used to compute the mean which we use as a normalization factor [17].

Mathematically, given an input image $I(x, y)$, the nine different edge, corner, and mean responses g_i can be computed by

$$g_i = I(x, y) * K_i, \qquad i = 1, 2, ..., 9 \tag{1}$$

Where $*$ represents a convolution operation. Fig. 4 shows an example of Frei-Chen kernels filtered images. In the figure, the upper row and the first image starting from the left in the middle row are the edge filtered images, the second four images are the corner filtered images, and the last one is the mean filtered image. All nine edge, corner, and mean responses g_i are extracted with their corresponding masks K_i for $i = 1, 2, ..., 9$ respectively.

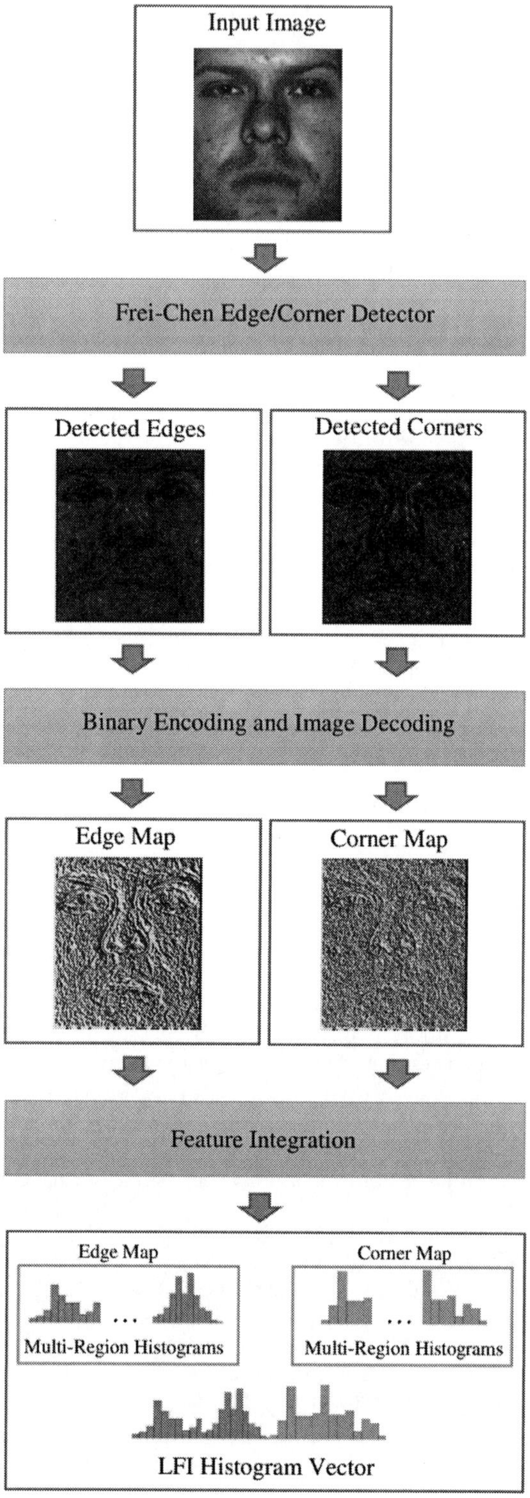

Figure 2. Overview of the proposed approach.

$$K_1 = \begin{bmatrix} 1 & \sqrt{2} & 1 \\ 0 & 0 & 0 \\ -1 & -\sqrt{2} & -1 \end{bmatrix} \quad K_2 = \begin{bmatrix} 1 & 0 & -1 \\ \sqrt{2} & 0 & -\sqrt{2} \\ 1 & 0 & -1 \end{bmatrix} \quad K_3 = \begin{bmatrix} 0 & -1 & \sqrt{2} \\ 1 & 0 & -1 \\ -\sqrt{2} & 1 & 0 \end{bmatrix}$$

$$K_4 = \begin{bmatrix} \sqrt{2} & -1 & 0 \\ -1 & 0 & 1 \\ 0 & 1 & -\sqrt{2} \end{bmatrix} \quad K_5 = \begin{bmatrix} 0 & 1 & 0 \\ -1 & 0 & -1 \\ 0 & 1 & 0 \end{bmatrix} \quad K_6 = \begin{bmatrix} -1 & 0 & 1 \\ 0 & 0 & 0 \\ 1 & 0 & -1 \end{bmatrix}$$

$$K_7 = \begin{bmatrix} 1 & -2 & 1 \\ -2 & 4 & -2 \\ 1 & -2 & 1 \end{bmatrix} \quad K_8 = \begin{bmatrix} -2 & 1 & -2 \\ 1 & 4 & 1 \\ -2 & 1 & -2 \end{bmatrix} \quad K_9 = \begin{bmatrix} 1 & 1 & 1 \\ 1 & 1 & 1 \\ 1 & 1 & 1 \end{bmatrix}$$

Figure 3. The nine Frei-Chen masks used to find the edge, corner, and mean responses of each image.

In terms of the edge detection denoted as E, we choose the first four filtered images g_i for $i = 1, ..., 4$ and project the image onto it. The projection equation can be given as

$$E = \sqrt{\frac{\sum_{i=1}^{4} g_i^2}{\sum_{i=1}^{9} g_i^2}} \tag{2}$$

When it comes to the corner detection that can be denoted as C, we choose the second four filtered images g_i for $i = 5, ..., 8$ and project the image onto it, which can be done by

$$C = \sqrt{\frac{\sum_{i=5}^{8} g_i^2}{\sum_{i=1}^{9} g_i^2}} \tag{3}$$

Fig. 5 shows the detected edges and corners after applying the two projection equations above.

B. Image Encoding and Decoding

After the edges and corners are detected separately as mentioned above, which can be seen in Fig. 5, a binary coding strategy is applied by exploiting the center pixel value in each 3×3 neighborhood regions, to encode the local structures information in the neighborhood. To form the edge or corner patterns, we compare each pixel with its neighboring pixels. If a neighbor pixel has a higher edge/corner value than the center pixel (or the same value) then a 1 is assigned to that pixel, which is otherwise a 0. The edge/corner binary code for that center pixel is produced by concatenating the eight $1s$ or $0s$. Finally, to retrieve the edge and corner features map, we change that binary codes into the corresponding decimal codes D, which can be defined as

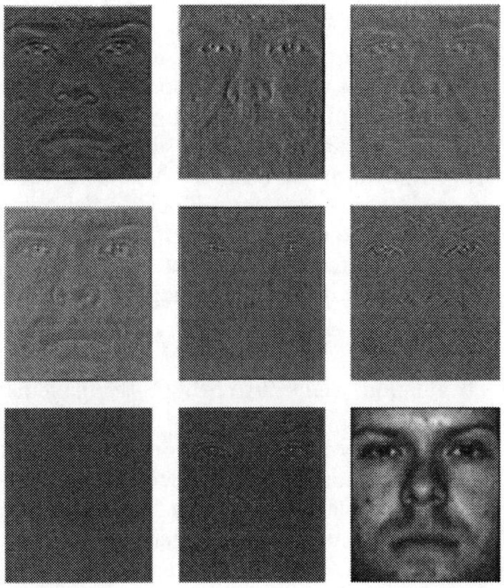

Figure 4. Projection of an image onto Frei-Chen edge, corner, and mean masks.

Figure 5. Edges and corners detected. Left input image, middle the detected edges, and right the detected corners.

$$D = \sum_{p=1}^{8} f(d_p - d_c) \times 2^{p-1} \tag{4}$$

and

$$f(x) = \begin{cases} 1 & \text{if } x \geq 0 \\ 0 & \text{if } x < 0 \end{cases} \tag{5}$$

where d_c and d_p denote the edge or corner values of the central pixel and its neighbors respectively. We use the detected edges image E and the detected corners image C, to generate a pattern for each pixel position. Fig. 6 shows a raw image, edge feature map, and the corner feature map after applying the binary coding and decoding strategy.

Figure 6. Coding and decoding strategy visualization. Left input image, middle the detected edges map, and right the detected corners map.

C. Feature Integration

To generate the final LFI feature vector, we map each edge/corner patterns to their corresponding histogram bin, then a 256 bin histogram would be computed for each edge and corner patterns separately. Finally, all the histograms will be concatenated to form the final LFI histogram vector for each input image. By this way, the LFI histogram contains all the information about the distribution of the local micro patterns such as edge, corener, line-end, flat, and spot, which can be used to statistically describe the image characteristics.

III. Experimental Results

For evaluation, we use two publicly available face datasets, named extended Yale B database [18][19] and AT&T (ORL) dataset [20]. In terms of the feature extraction process, to consider the local information of face components, we divide each image into small blocks as can be seen in Fig. 7. After that, we extract the information of each block separately using our proposed technique LFI and represent it as a local LFI histogram. Finally, we concatenate these local histograms to form a global histogram for each input image that contains information about the distribution of the local micro-patterns of the image, and can be used to statistically describe the face image characteristics. The length of this feature vector (global histogram) depends on the number of blocks (regions) of each image.

When it comes to the face recognition process, the objective is to compare the encoded feature vector from one image with all other candidate feature vectors of the dataset using two different method for classification. The first one, is a library for support vector machines (LIBSVM) [21], and the second one is, chi-square metric χ^2, which is a measure between two feature vectors, $H1$ and $H2$, of length N, that can be defined as

$$\chi^2(H_1, H_2) = \sum_{i=1}^{N} \frac{(H_1(i) - H_2(i))^2}{H_1(i) + H_2(i) + \epsilon} \tag{6}$$

where ϵ is a very small value that used to avoid division by 0.

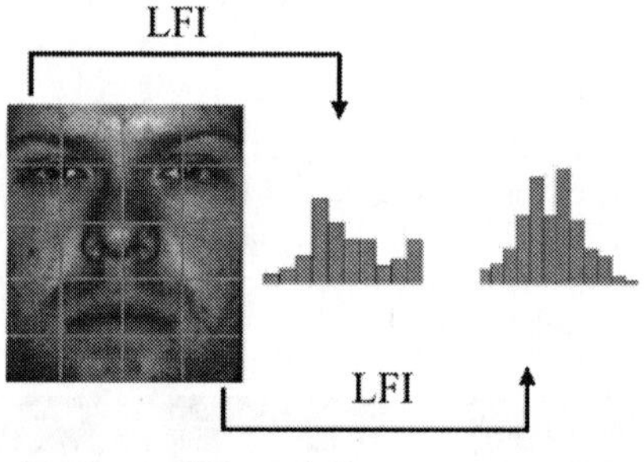

Figure 7. A face images is divided into small blocks and the features are extracted using LFI and a histogram is built for each area. Then all the histograms are concatenated.

A. Extended Yale B Database

The extended Yale B database has a total of 2280 face images for 38 subjects representing 60 illumination conditions per subject under the frontal pose, all the images resized to 64×64. Fig. 8 shows sample faces of this dataset. In the figure, from the bottom raw it is hard even for human being to recognize the person in some cases, especially the right bottom sample we cannot even say if there is a face or any other object in the image. Fig.s 9 and 10 show the edge and corner map of the face images in Fig. 8. It is clear that using Frei-Chen edge/corner detector, the edges and corners in dark areas of the image are likely to be detected. Therefore, the illumination variation problems will be overcome, which significantly helps to improve the face recognition performance under uncontrolled illumination/lighting environments.

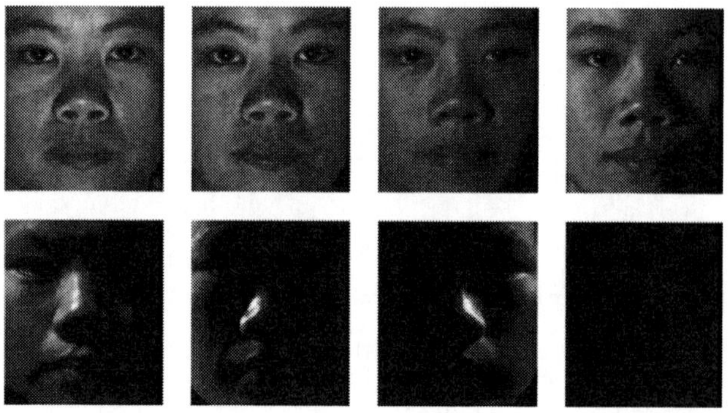

Figure 8. Samples of one subject from the Extended Yale B database.

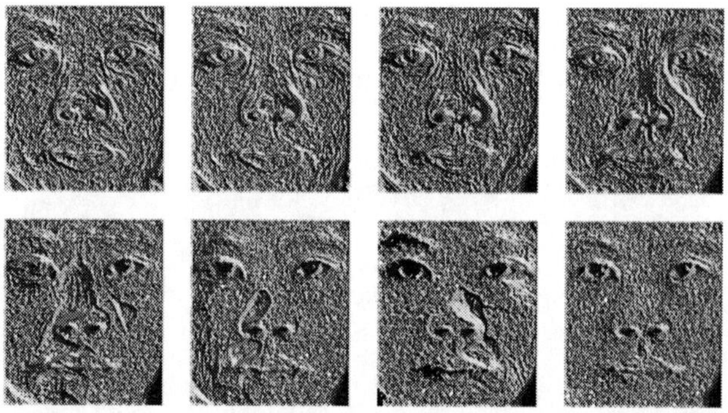

Figure 9. LFI edge map of one subject from the Extended Yale B database.

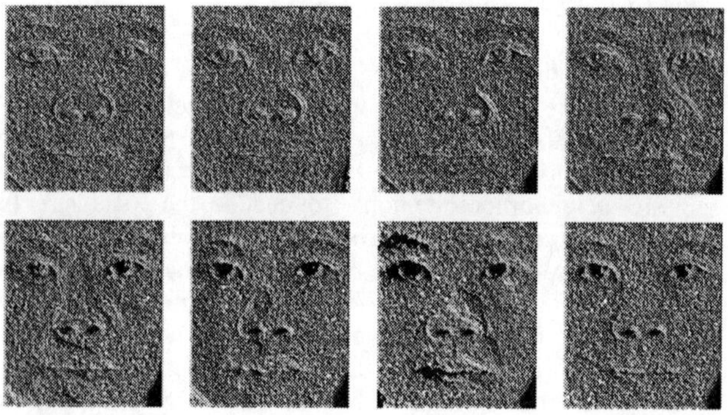

Figure 10. LFI corner map of one subject from the Extended Yale B database.

To avoid any bias, by using the χ^2 we select one image per subject of the data for training and the rest of the data for testing. The experiments were repeated 60 times as there are a total of 60 samples/subject, then the average results are calculated. On the other hand, by using $LIBSVM$ we randomly select half of the data for training and the other half for testing. The experiments were repeated 30 times, then the average results are calculated for comparison. The performance results of well known face recognition algorithms like local ternary patterns (LTP) [22], Weber-face [23] and gradientface (GradFace) [24], as well as LBP and LDP [16], with the proposed method on extended Yale B dataset are presented in Table I. Note that, the results we compared with are as we got from their original references which are mentioned in the table. Meanwhile, part of the extended Yale B dataset (standard Yale B dataset) was used in [23][24].

TABLE I. PERFORMANCE RESULTS OF WELL KNOWN FACE RECOGNITION ALGORITHMS TOGETHER WITH THE PROPOSED METHOD ON EXTENDED YALE B DATASET.

Refernce	Method	Highest Recognition Accuracy
Proposed	LFI / LIBSVM	**99.29 %**
Proposed	LFI / χ^2	**99.24 %**
[24]	GradFace	98.96 %
[22]	RLTP	98.71 %
[23]	Weber-face	98.30 %
[22]	LTP	98.25 %
[24]	LTV	97.93 %
[16]	LDP+2D-PCA	96.43 %
[22]	LBP	96.07 %
[16]	LBP+2D-PCA	91.54 %
[16]	LDP+PCA	81.34 %

B. AT&T Dataset (ORL)

The ORL database contains a total of 400 face images corresponding to 10 different images of 40 distinct subjects. Some sample faces are shown in Fig. 11. The images are taken at different times with different specifications, including slightly varying in illumination, different facial expressions such as open and closed eyes, smiling and non-smiling, and facial details like wearing glasses. All the images resized to 64×64. Table II summarizes the highest recognition rates of the proposed local edge/corner feature integration method compared to well known face recognition algorithms together like (GLCM+LDP+EDGE) [25], and State Preserving Extreme Learning Machine (SPELM) [26], and a combined phase congruency and Gabor wavelet techniques (PC/GW) [27], as well as LBP and LDP, with the proposed method on ORL dataset with the use of χ^2 similarity measure and $LIBSVM$. Note that, the results we compared with are as we got from their original references which are mentioned in the table, since we do not have any original codes of of these algorithms. The procedure of splitting the training and testing data has been done as in the previous experiment. Therefore, we select one image per subject of the data for training and the rest of the data for testing to avoid any bias. The experiments were repeated 10 times, then the average results were calculated for comparison using χ^2. Additionally, we select seven images of the data randomly for training the $LIBSVM$ classifier and the rest for testing. The experiments were repeated 10 times, then the average results were calculated.

Figure 11. Samples of a subject from the ORL database

TABLE II. PERFORMANCE RESULTS OF WELL KNOWN FACE RECOGNITION ALGORITHMS TOGETHER WITH THE PROPOSED METHOD ON ORL DATASET.

Refernce	Method	Highest Recognition Accuracy
Proposed	LFI / LIBSVM	**99.17 %**
Proposed	LFI / χ^2	**98.88 %**
[25]	GLCM+LDP+EDGE	98.75 %
[27]	GW+PC+PCA	98.00 %
[27]	GW+PC	98.00 %
[26]	Gabor+SPELM	97.97 %
[25]	LDP+EDGE	96.60 %
[25]	GLCM+LDP	92.70 %
[26]	PHOG+SPELM	92.45 %
[25]	GLCM+EDGE	90.50 %
[25]	LDP	88.50 %
[27]	PCA	88.00 %
[25]	LBP	87.80 %

IV. CONCLUSION

In this paper, we have introduced a new feature descriptor technique named local edge/corner feature integration. Throughout the performance evaluation, we found that LFI is robust for face recognition regardless of extremely variations of illumination/lighting environments as in extended Yale B database, and slightly differences of pose conditions as in AT&T dataset. In addition, compared to the other state-of-the-art methods, we can say that our method provides better accuracy in most test cases. From the results above, it is clear that the LFI provides a stronger discriminative capability in describing detailed texture information than the LBP and LDP. In general, considering all comparison results, we can assess that LFI can be a promising candidate for face recognition applications. The work is progressing to investigate the ability of the proposed technique LFI with different applications such as dynamic texture recognition.

REFERENCES

[1] T. Mäenpää and M. Pietikäinen, "Texture analysis with local binary patterns," Handbook of Pattern Recognition and Computer Vision, vol. 3, pp. 197–216, 2005.

[2] T. Ojala, M. Pietikäinen, and D. Harwood, "A comparative study of texture measures with classification based on featured distributions," Pattern recognition, vol. 29, no. 1, pp. 51–59, 1996.

[3] T. Ahonen, A. Hadid, and M. Pietikäinen, "Face recognition with local binary patterns, computer vision, eccv 2004 proceedings," Lecture Notes in Computer Science, vol. 3021, pp. 469–481, 2004.

[4] A. Hadid, M. Pietikainen, and T. Ahonen, "A discriminative feature space for detecting and recognizing faces," in Computer Vision and Pattern Recognition, 2004. CVPR 2004. Proceedings of the 2004 IEEE Computer Society Conference on, vol. 2. IEEE, pp. II–797, 2004.

[5] D. Huijsman and N. Sebe, "Content-based indexing performance: A class size normalized precision," in Recall, Generality Evaluation, International Conference on Image Processing (ICIP'03), vol. 3, pp. 733–736, 2003.

[6] D. Grangier and S. Bengio, "A discriminative kernel-based approach to rank images from text queries," IEEE transactions on pattern analysis and machine intelligence, vol. 30, no. 8, pp. 1371–1384, 2008.

[7] W. Ali, F. Georgsson, and T. Hellstrom, "Visual tree detection for autonomous navigation in forest environment," in Intelligent Vehicles Symposium, 2008 IEEE. IEEE, pp. 560–565, 2008.

[8] L. Nanni and A. Lumini, "Ensemble of multiple pedestrian representations," IEEE Transactions on Intelligent Transportation Systems, vol. 9, no. 2, pp. 365–369, 2008.

[9] T. Mäenpää, J. Viertola, and M. Pietikäinen, "Optimising colour and texture features for real-time visual inspection," Pattern Analysis & Applications, vol. 6, no. 3, pp. 169–175, 2003.

[10] M. Turtinen, M. Pietikainen, and O. SilvÉn, "Visual characterization of paper using isomap and local binary patterns," IEICE transactions on information and systems, vol. 89, no. 7, pp. 2076–2083, 2006.

[11] M. Heikkila and M. Pietikainen, "A texture-based method for modeling the background and detecting moving objects," IEEE transactions on pattern analysis and machine intelligence, vol. 28, no. 4, pp. 657–662, 2006.

[12] V. Kellokumpu, G. Zhao, and M. Pietikäinen, "Human activity recognition using a dynamic texture based method." in BMVC, vol. 1, p. 2, 2008.

[13] A. Oliver, X. Lladó, J. Freixenet, and J. Martí, "False positive reduction in mammographic mass detection using local binary patterns," in International Conference on Medical Image Computing and Computer-Assisted Intervention. Springer, pp. 286–293, 2007.

[14] S. Kluckner, G. Pacher, H. Grabner, H. Bischof, and J. Bauer, "A 3d teacher for car detection in aerial images," in 2007 IEEE 11th International Conference on Computer Vision. IEEE, pp. 1–8, 2007.

[15] T. Jabid, M. H. Kabir, and O. Chae, "Robust facial expression recognition based on local directional pattern," ETRI journal, vol. 32, no. 5, pp. 784–794, 2010.

[16] D.-J. Kim, S.-H. Lee, and M.-K. Sohn, "Face recognition via local directional pattern," International Journal of Security and Its Applications, vol. 7, no. 2, pp. 191–200, 2013.

[17] W. Frei and C.-C. Chen, "Fast boundary detection: A generalizationand new algorithm," IEEE Transactions on Computers, vol. 26, no. 10, 1977.

[18] A. S. Georghiades and P. N. Belhumeur, "Illumination cone models for faces recognition under variable lighting," in Proceedings of CVPR98, 1998.

[19] K.-C. Lee, J. Ho, and D. J. Kriegman, "Acquiring linear subspaces for face recognition under variable lighting," Pattern Analysis and Machine Intelligence, IEEE Transactions on, vol. 27, no. 5, pp. 684–698, 2005.

[20] F. S. Samaria and A. C. Harter, "Parameterisation of a stochastic model for human face identification," in Applications of Computer Vision, 1994., Proceedings of the Second IEEE Workshop on. IEEE, pp. 138–142, 1994.

[21] C.-C. Chang and C.-J. Lin, "Libsvm: a library for support vector machines," ACM Transactions on Intelligent Systems and Technology (TIST), vol. 2, no. 3, p. 27, 2011.

[22] J. Ren, X. Jiang, and J. Yuan, "Relaxed local ternary pattern for face recognition." in ICIP, pp. 3680–3684, 2013.

[23] B. Wang, W. Li, W. Yang, and Q. Liao, "Illumination normalization based on weber's law with application to face recognition," IEEE Signal Processing Letters, vol. 18, no. 8, pp. 462–465, 2011.

[24] T. Zhang, Y. Y. Tang, B. Fang, Z. Shang, and X. Liu, "Face recognition under varying illumination using gradientfaces," IEEE Transactions on Image Processing, vol. 18, no. 11, pp. 2599–2606, 2009.

[25] A. Kar, D. Bhattacharjee, D. K. Basu, M. Nasipuri, and M. Kundu, "An adaptive block based integrated ldp, glcm, and morphological features for face recognition," arXiv preprint arXiv:1312.1512, 2013.

[26] M. Z. Alom, P. Sidike, V. K. Asari, and T. M. Taha, "State preserving extreme learning machine for face recognition," in 2015 International Joint Conference on Neural Networks (IJCNN). IEEE, pp. 1–7, 2015.

[27] E. Bezalel and U. Efron, "Efficient face recognition method using a combined phase congruency/gabor wavelet technique," in Optics & Photonics 2005. International Society for Optics and Photonics, pp. 59 081K–59 081K, 2005.

Approximating Imprecise Planar Tesselations with Voronoi Diagrams

Narciso Aguilera
PhD Program
University of Valladolid, Spain
and Univ. Nacional de Ingeniería,
Managua, Nicaragua
Email: njaguilera@uni.edu.ni

Belén Palop
Didáctica de la Matemática
Departmento de Didáctica
University of Valladolid
Segovia, Spain
Email: bpalop@infor.uva.es

Hebert Pérez-Rosés
Department of Mathematics
University of Lleida, Spain
and conjoint fellow
Univ. of Newcastle, Australia
Email: hebert.perez@gmail.com

Abstract—**Natural growth processes tend to generate shapes in the form of imprecise planar tesselations, where the tiles do not match exactlyand leave some space among them. In this paper we model these tesselations by means of Voronoi Diagrams. We look for the set of 2D-sites whose Voronoi Diagram better approximates the given imprecise tessellation. Since we conjecture the Inverse Voronoi Problem (also known as Voronoi-fitting Problem) to be NP-hard, we describe in this paper a heuristic algorithm that looks for the optimal set of sites.. We study the algorithm's performance and validity on a set of tesselations extracted from real-life images. With the aid of these experiments, we find optimal values for a tunable parameter of the algorithm. In the long run, our main goal is to develop a tool that can automatically analize an image of a tessellation that is expected to be modelled with a Voronoi Diagram (e.g., pictures from chrystals, trees in a forest, etc), and decide whether the growth process was or was not affected by some external force. This inverse computation should be able tell how far is the image from its theoretical model.**

Keywords–Planar tesselations; Voronoi Diagram; local search; Inverse Voronoi Diagram.

I. Introduction

Voronoi Diagrams (or Dirichlet tesselations) are a fundamental geometric structure with many applications in Graphics and Image Processing, among other uses. Informally, the Voronoi Diagram generated by a set S of points in the Euclidean plane is a subdivision of the plane into (convex) cells, where each cell is associated with one point $p \in S$, and consists of the points on the plane that are closer to p than to any other $q \in S$. In other words, the cell associated with some point p can be thought of as a sort of *sphere of influence* of p. For the precise definition, as well as the most important properties of Voronoi Diagrams, we refer the reader to any one of the many standard texts on the subject, such as [1].

The above definition lends itself very naturally to many generalizations, such as using sites other than points, considering metrics other than the Euclidean metric, dimensions higher than two, or surfaces other than the plane. Since many growth processes in nature follow this very simple model, in this paper, we will restrict ourselves to the Euclidean plane, the Euclidean metric and point sites. In fact, due to the applied focus of this paper, we will restrict the area of study to a bounded rectangle in the 2D-plane where the tessellation is given, and perform the algorithm's adjustments using real-life image pictures.

Planar Euclidean Voronoi Diagrams have been applied to describe images and other visual or spatial patterns since the late 1970s [2], [3] and [4]. In particular, [2] attempts to approximate a cellular pattern by a Voronoi Diagram and this is, to the best of our knowledge the first reference to what we now call *the Inverse Voronoi Problem*. In this paper, we present an algorithm that focuses on finding how a picture, that looks like a Voronoi Diagram to the naked eye, can (or cannot) be approximated by that model. We conjecture that finding the model that better approximates the final picture of a growth process can give useful information on how the process itself happened and if unforseen external circumstances may have altered it. The Inverse Voronoi Problem (IVP) can be stated as follows:

Problem 1 (Inverse Voronoi Problem): Given a Voronoi Tesselation T in the Euclidean Plane, find the set of points P that generate T.

After [2], this problem was addressed again in [5] and [6]. The approach followed by Suzuki and Iri in [6] is similar to that of [2]: their aim is to find a Voronoi Diagram that best approximates the tesselation T, according to some measure of approximation. On the other hand, in [5] Ash and Bolker try to find the Voronoi Diagram that fits T *exactly*. Unfortunately, this is not always possible, since not every tesselation T corresponds exactly to a Voronoi Diagram, even if all the cells of T are convex.

In this paper, we continue along the lines of [2] and [6]: We consider a relaxation of the concept of planar tesselation, and we devise an algorithm that tries to find the Voronoi Diagram that best approximates this relaxed tesselation.

In a standard tesselation of the plane, the tiles cover the entire plane, and their intersection is a set of *edges*, with measure zero. However, this ideal situation does not correspond to reality in many cases. In many actual spatial patterns, including images, the cell boundaries may have some thickness, or to put it in another way, the tiles do not match exactly, leaving some space between them. This situation was recently considered in [7], where the Voronoi edges have some constant width $w > 0$. In this paper, we consider a more general situation, which we may call *imprecise planar tesselation*.

Definition 1 (Imprecise planar tesselations): An imprecise (or incomplete) tesselation of a bounded region $R \subseteq \mathbb{R}^2$ is a set $\mathcal{P}$ of polygons, or tiles (not necessarily convex), such that each $P \in \mathcal{P}$ is strictly contained in R, has a non-empty interior; and $\bigcap_{P \in \mathcal{P}} P$ has zero measure.

Note that we preserve the condition that the intersection between cells has zero measure, but we do not require that $\bigcup_{P \in \mathcal{P}} P$ covers the entire Euclidean plane $\mathbb{R}^2$, hence $\mathcal{P}$ is not a tesselation in the usual sense. The set $R - \bigcup_{P \in \mathcal{P}} P$ will be called *the grey area*. When we try to approximate $\mathcal{P}$ by a Voronoi Diagram, we care about where each $P \in \mathcal{P}$ lies with respect to the Voronoi Diagram, but we are indifferent as to where some part of the grey area goes.

Section II describes the heuristic algorithm to approximate planar imprecise tesselations. In Section III, we give examples of imprecise tesselations of the plane taken from real-life applications, and we run the algorithm with those tesselations, in order to analyze its performance. From these experiments, we draw conclusions regarding a certain tunable parameter of the aforementioned algorithm. Please note that, since this is a Work In Progress, the obtained values and the decisions made in order to tune our algorithm are still subject to further research.

II. APPROXIMATING IMPRECISE TESSELATIONS

In the following, we will assume that $\mathcal{P}$ consists of n polygons $\{P_1, \dots P_n\}$, and our aim is to approximate it by a Voronoi Diagram $\mathcal{V}$ with exactly n cells $\{V_1, \dots V_n\}$, i.e. one per polygon. For each $1 \leq i \leq n$, the Voronoi cell V_i should cover the tile P_i as much as possible, and perhaps some of the gray area, but should refrain from invading any other tile P_j, with $j \neq i$.

Using the area of the missclasified region as a measure of the fitness of a candidate solution, we can define our goal as follows: For each Voronoi cell V_i, we compute the area of the portions of polygons in $\mathcal{P}$ other than P_i that lie inside V_i. The sum of the areas of all regions for each $1 \leq i \leq n$ is the area of the missclasified region. (Note that the portions of P_i that do not belong to V_i will be counted when the containing Voronoi cell is processed.)

Since we will, in practice, never work with the entire plane but with a bounded region, typically a rectangular section R, if $a(X)$ represents the area of a polygon X, we may define the *normalized unwanted area* of $\mathcal{V}$, relative to $\mathcal{P}$, as follows:

$$\begin{aligned} \Upsilon_{\mathcal{P}}(\mathcal{V}) &= \frac{1}{a(R)} \sum_{i=1}^{n} (a(P_i) - a(P_i \cap V_i)) \\ &= \frac{1}{a(R)} \sum_{i=1}^{n} a(P_i) - \frac{1}{a(R)} \sum_{i=1}^{n} a(P_i \cap V_i) \end{aligned} \tag{1}$$

Hence, we treat the problem of approximating $\mathcal{P}$ as an optimization problem, where we have to minimize the objective function Υ, which in general, is a non-linear and non-differentiable function. Note that the first term of (1), i.e. $\frac{1}{a(R)} \sum_{i=1}^{n} a(P_i)$, is constant, therefore, minimizing Υ amounts to maximizing the term $\sum_{i=1}^{n} a(P_i \cap V_i)$.

In order to minimize Υ, we may use any of the well-known heuristics developed for non-linear optimization, such as any variant of local search, simulated annealing, genetic algorithms, etc. (see [8], for instance). In this paper, we settle for a simple variant of local search, which is roughly described in the algorithm in Fig. 1 as a first attempt to explore the solution space. We will also see that looking for this minimum is not an easy task and that, being the optimal location for each point dependant on every point other than itself, careful tuning needs to be performed in order not to *fall* in a local minimum. Starting with the centroids of the tiles, the algorithm is going to try to move one site at a time in any of the 8 main directions.

Input: An imprecise tesselation $\mathcal{P} = \{P_1, \dots P_n\}$, an approximation ϵ.
Output: A set of sites $S = \{s_1, \dots s_n\}$ whose Voronoi Diagram approximates $\mathcal{P}$.

▷ Compute First Candidate Solution
for each polygon $P_i \in \mathcal{P}$ **do**
    $s_i \leftarrow$ centroid of P_i
end for
$\mathcal{V} \leftarrow$ Voronoi Diagram generated by S
$A \leftarrow \Upsilon_{\mathcal{P}}(\mathcal{V})$
▷ Improve the solution
while solution still improving **do**
    for each site $s_i \in S$ **do**
        for each direction {N,NE,E,SE,S,SW,W,NS} **do**
            $s'_i \leftarrow$ translation(s_i,direction,distance)
            candidate $\leftarrow S$ with s'_i instead of s_i
            $\mathcal{V}' \leftarrow$ Voronoi Diagram(candidate)
            $A' \leftarrow \Upsilon_{\mathcal{P}}(\mathcal{V}')$
            $(s^*_i, A^*) \leftarrow$ best among all directions
        end for
        $s_i \leftarrow s^*_i$; $A = A^*$
    end for
    if solution not improving **then**
        distance $\leftarrow$ some factor of distance
    end if
end while

Figure 1. Voronoi Approximation of Imprecise Tesselation

The best among these positions for that particular site, will be chosen and the site will be reassigned to that location. We iterate this process until no site in the current solution can be moved. When this happens, we decrease the distance that we are going to test, looking for locations that are closer to the site. Since we don't expect real-world Voronoi Diagrams to be centroidal, at the beginning, farther positions from the centroid are explored. As the algorithm proceeds, the sites tend to get closer to the optimal location and smaller steps are given. We will see in Section III that how we reduce the distance in those tests, drastically affects the final solution and the running times.

Algorithm in Fig. 1 shows the main idea that we have followed in order to implement the descent method for our problem. Even though many different approaches can be tested and small modifications can slightly improve the final result or the computational time, we describe here the main decisions that have been taken in order to optimize a given imprecise tesellation.

- A candidate solution is found when translating one site in the previous candidate solution. Note that this movement has a direct effect on all Voronoi neighbouring cells and, in the long run, might force the move of any other site in S.
- Translation vectors have been carefully studied showing that 8 directions give good enough approximations in practical cases.
- Translation distance happens to be one of the most important parameters, showing our results that both optimization and performance benefit from a distance reduction by some factor each time the algorithm gets

stuck in a local minimum for the present distance.

- The algorithm terminates when the improvements in the normalized unwanted area is smaller than ϵ after several attempts.

We have implemented and tested several variations on this algorithm in order to find a good balance between achieving a good approximation and the computational time needed to obtain it. Note that, whenever a new candidate solution is tested, the whole Voronoi Diagram might have to be recomputed. We briefly discuss in the following the choices that we have made in our implementation and justify them according to our experimental results:

- If site s_i moves in along a certain direction in one iteration, we have seen that it is very probable that the same direction will be chosen in the next move. Therefore, we have also implemented versions for the algorithm where not all 8 directions are tested, but we move a site if the same direction as the previous iteration already gives an improvement without needing to test the other 7 directions. This choice does reach similar results in the approximation bounds while being more efficient.
- Once all sites are tested and no movement is found to improve the present solution, we decrease the distance for the translation (which will be proportional to its distance to its nearest neighbour). Intuitively, this process allows the points to approach fast their best location and improve within that location afterwards.
- Even though when we approach the best location improvements tend to be small, this condition might be also met during the whole process. We establish the number of rounds in which we will already consider that no further improvement is expected.

III. Computational experiments

In order to test the performance of Algorithm 1 we have chosen some imprecise tesselations, obtained by segmenting real-life images coming from different domains.

The example, Fig. 2 [9] shows a honeycomb, which is an almost perfect hexagonal tiling of the plane. With this image, since the Voronoi Diagram originating perfect hexagonal tilings is centroidal (i.e. generators lie on the centroids of the cells), the objective function is essentially minimized at the initialization step. On the other hand, we have several non-centroidal Voronoi tesselation of the plane. Fig. 3 [10] is a microscopic image of common waterweed, Canadian pondweed (*Elodea canadensis*), an aquatic plant from North America. Fig. 4 [11] is another microscopic image, from a metal's crystalline structure. Finally, Fig. 5 [12] is a satellite image of a farming area in Oxfordshire, UK. Despite the limits between farms not appearing through a natural growth process, their resemblance to a Voronoi Diagram is remarkable (In the best run, $\Upsilon = 4.6\%$, even smaller than our best run for the crystal structure).

All the aforementioned images show a clear pattern of tiles that tesselate the plane in an imprecise manner. We have segmented the images in order to obtain imprecise planar tesselations and, for each one of these tesselations, we have run our algorithm with different step reduction factors. For each experiment, we have measured the number of iterations, the running times and the initial and the final values of the

Figure 2. Original Honeycomb picture (top), VD for centroids (left) and optimal VD after running the algorithm (right).

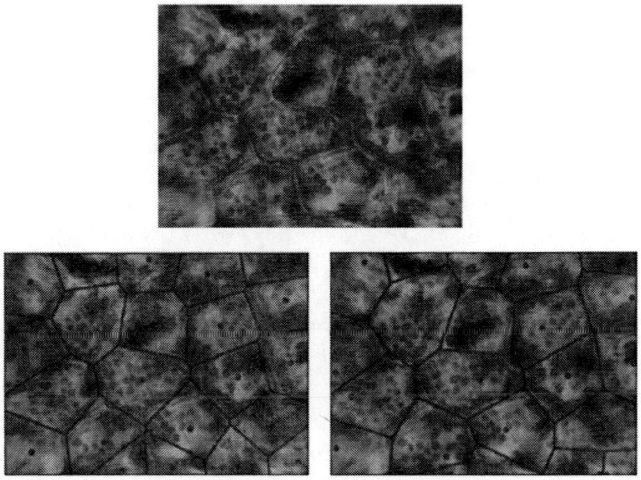

Figure 3. Original Cells of Elodea canadensis picture (top), VD for centroids (left) and optimal VD after running the algorithm (right).

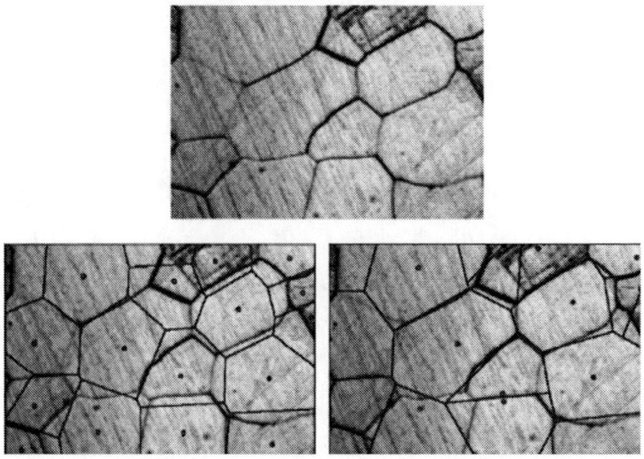

Figure 4. Original Crystal grain picture (top), VD for centroids (left) and optimal VD after running the algorithm (right).

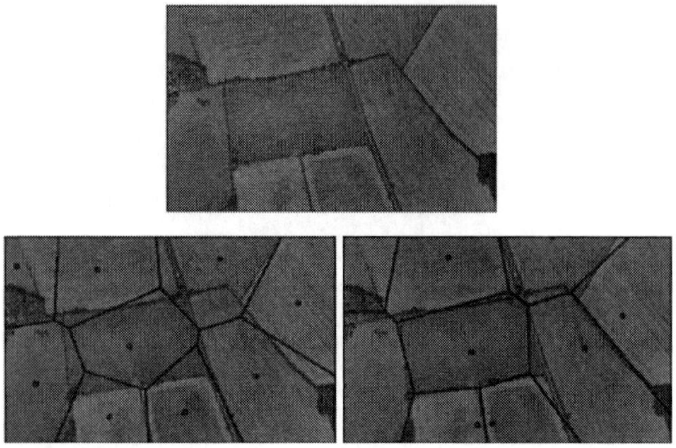

Figure 5. Original Farmland plateau in Oxfordshire (UK) picture (top), VD for centroids (left) and optimal VD after running the algorithm (right).

objective function. We have randomized the order in which the sites are processed in each loop. Even though neither the running times nor the optimal solution is dramatically affected by this randomness, we have run the algorithm ten times for each distance factor, and have taken the average of these ten values for each parameter. In each case we have also computed the relative cost, which is the number of iterations that are necessary to gain one percentage point of accuracy in the approximation. Tables I, II and III contain the results of those measurements. The experiments have been carried out on a personal computer equipped with an Intel Core i5 processor, with 8 GB RAM, running under Windows 10 and the algorithm has been implemented using the R language.

TABLE I. COMPUTATIONAL RESULTS FOR FIG. 3

Initial Υ	10.6%						
Step reduction	0.05	0.15	0.30	0.50	0.70	0.85	0.95
# iterations	228	139	122	115	108	74	3
Time (secs.)	210	122	132	163	238	299	104
Final Υ	7.4%	6.5%	5.5%	5.1%	4.7%	5.8%	9.8%
Relative cost	71.2	33.9	23.9	20.9	18.3	15.4	3.7

TABLE II. COMPUTATIONAL RESULTS FOR FIG. 4

Initial Υ	20.4%						
Step reduction	0.05	0.15	0.30	0.50	0.70	0.85	0.95
# iterations	266	117	119	98	102	59	1
Time (s)	204	91	107	130	216	247	49
Final Υ	16.4%	16.2%	13.3%	12%	10.6%	13%	20%
Relative cost	66.5	28	16.7	11.6	10.6	7.8	2.5

TABLE III. COMPUTATIONAL RESULTS FOR FIG. 5

Initial Υ	11.1%						
Step reduction	0.05	0.15	0.30	0.50	0.70	0.85	0.95
# iterations	238	59	59	59	46	14	0
Time (secs.)	91	23	27	34	46	33	10
Final Υ	6.6%	7.5%	6.3%	5%	4.6%	8.1%	11.1%
Relative cost	53	16.4	12.2	9.6	7	4.6	— —

Fig. 6 shows the degree of approximation achieved by Algorithm 1 for the images above. Although the level of approximation varies substantially from one image to another, note that the maximum approximation is attained in all cases with a step reduction factor approximately equal to 0.7.

Besides the degree of approximation, we are also interested in the amount of work done to achieve the desired approximation. Fig. 7 makes a graphical comparison of the relative cost

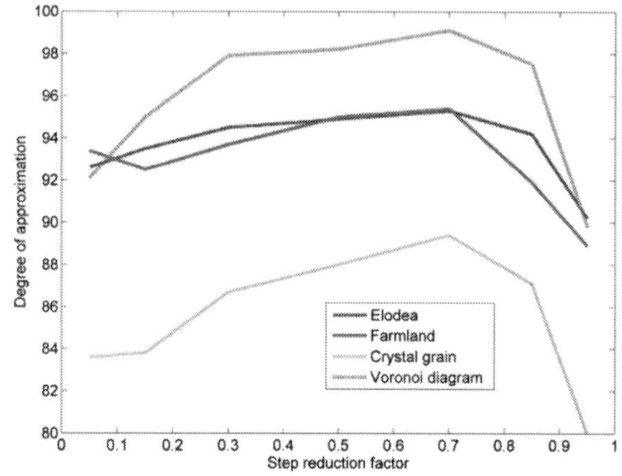

Figure 6. Degree of approximation as a function of the step reduction factor

computed in Tables I, II, and III. Note that the minimum cost is attained in all cases when the step reduction factor approaches 1.

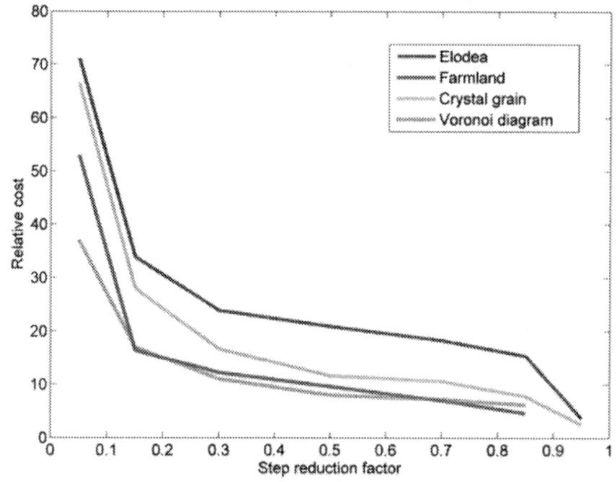

Figure 7. Relative cost as a function of the step reduction factor

IV. CONCLUSIONS AND FUTURE WORK

In this paper we have introduced the concept of imprecise planar tesselation, in order to model images arising in many practical situations. Our experiments show that imprecise planar tesselations can be approximated quite accurately with the aid of Voronoi Diagrams, which provides a nice geometric model for several types of images. Moreover, we have detected a coincidence in relation with the step reduction factor: in all four images, the best approximation is achieved when the step reduction factor is approximately equal to 0.7, and the algorithm performs more efficiently with a larger step reduction factor, although the approximation decreases sharply. This gives us some rough guidelines for tuning the step reduction factor, depending on our priorities at each moment. As a rule of thumb, a step reduction factor between 0.7 and 0.75 seems to be a good choice, leaning towards 0.7 if we want more accuracy, or towards 0.75 if we need more efficiency. However, these guidelines have to be confirmed by more extensive experiments.

There are many ways to improve our method for approximating imprecise planar tesselations. We can replace our algorithm by a more sophisticated metaheuristic, such as simulated annealing, or an evolutionary algorithm. Another improvement may be derived by considering a more general variant of the Inverse Voronoi Problem, where we would allow more than one Voronoi cell per tile. This *Generalized Inverse Voronoi Problem* has already been considered before in [13] and [14], for instance, but these two papers have focused on the *exact* version of the problem only. The approximated version might yield better results, in the sense that a reasonably good aproximation might be found with far fewer Voronoi generators than those used in [13] and [14].

ACKNOWLEDGMENTS

Narciso Aguilera is supported by an EURICA PhD scholarship for Latin American students. The EURICA program is coordinated by the University of Groningen, the Netherlands, together with several associated universities in Europe and Latin America. Belen Palop has been partially supported by project MTM2015-63791-R. Hebert Pérez-Rosés acknowledges partial support from project MTM2013-46949-P, funded by the Spanish Ministry for Economy and Competitiveness (MINECO). The authors would like to thank Manuel Abellanas (Universidad Politécnica de Madrid) for the fruitful discussions and ongoing research on this problem.

REFERENCES

[1] A. Okabe, B. Boots, K. Sugihara, and S. Chiu, Spatial Tesselations: Concepts and Applications of Voronoi Diagrams. John Wiley and Sons, 2000.

[2] H. Honda, "Description of Cellular Patterns by Dirichlet Domains: The Two-Dimensional Case," Journal of Theoretical Biology, vol. 72, pp. 523–543, 1978.

[3] N. Ahuja, B. An, and B. Schachter, "Image Representation using Voronoi Tesselation," Computer Vision, Graphics and Image Processing, vol. 29, pp. 286–295, 1985.

[4] M. Tanemura, "Statistical Distributions of Poisson Voronoi Cells in Two and Three Dimensions," Forma, vol. 18, pp. 221–247, 2003.

[5] M. M. Ash and E. D. Bolker, "Recognizing Dirichlet Tesselations," Geometriae Dedicata, vol. 19, pp. 175–206, 1985.

[6] A. Suzuki and M. Iri, "Approximation of a tessellation of the plane by a Voronoi diagram," Journal of the Operations Research Society of Japan, vol. 29, pp. 69–96, 1986.

[7] M. Ferraro and L. Zaninetti, "On the statistics of area size in two-dimensional thick Voronoi diagrams," Physica A, vol. 391, pp. 4575–4582, 2012.

[8] T. Gonzalez, Ed., Handbook of Approximation Algorithms and Metaheuristics. Chapman and Hall - CRC, 2007.

[9] "Pixabay," 2016, URL: https://pixabay.com/es/panal-las-abejas-hex%C3%A1gonos-peine-330755 [accessed: 2016-01-02]

[10] Howard Sidney Thomas — Cell senescence, 2016, URL: http://www.sidthomas.net/SenEssence/Evolution/cellsen.htm [accessed: 2016-01-02].

[11] Wikimedia commons — File: CrystalGrain.jpg, 2016, URL: https://commons.wikimedia.org/wiki/File:CrystalGrain.jpg [accessed: 2016-01-02]

[12] Oxforshire county council — Landscape Types: Farmland Plateau Aerial View, 2016, URL: http://owls.oxfordshire.gov.uk/wps/wcm/connect/occ/OWLS/Home/Oxfordshire+Landscape+Types/Farmland+Plateau/Farmland+Plateau+Aerial+View [accessed: 2016-01-02].

[13] S. Banerjee et al., "On the Construction of a Generalized Voronoi Inverse of a Rectangular Tesselation," in Proceedings of the 9th Int. IEEE Symp. on Voronoi Diagrams in Science and Engineering, June 27–29, 2012, New Brunswick, NJ, USA. IEEE, pp. 132–137, 2012.

[14] G. Aloupis, H. Pérez-Rosés, G. Pineda-Villavicencio, P. Taslakian, and D. Trinchet, "Fitting Voronoi Diagrams to Planar Tesselations," Lecture Notes in Computer Science, vol. 8288, pp. 349–361, 2013.

Incremental Reconstruction of Moving Object Trajectory

Muhammad Majid Afzal
Decibel Insight
London, UK
email: admtel@gmail.com

Prof. Karim Ouazzane, Dr. Vassil Vassilev, Yogesh Patel
Cyber Security Research Group, School of Computing and Digital Media, London Metropolitan University, London, UK
email: {k.ouazzane, v.vassilev, y.patel}@londonmet.ac.uk

Abstract—**This article presents a model and a prototype implementation of a technical application programming interface (API) for incremental reconstruction of the moving objects trajectories captured by closed-circuit television (CCTV) and High-definition television (HDTV) cameras. This paper proposes a unique, much simpler model-driven approach which is more efficient than other approaches for dynamic tracking such as Microsoft Kinect. The research reported here is part of a research program of the Cybersecurity Research Group of London Metropolitan University for real-time video analytics with applicability to surveillance in security, disaster recovery and safety management, and customer insight.**

Keywords: Video surveillance; Real-time video analytics; Moving objects tracking; Trajectory reconstruction; Model-driven motion description; Incremental algorithms.

I. INTRODUCTION

Intelligent and prompt moving object tracking is a difficult issue in the computer vision research area. Multiple objects tracking has many useful applications in scene analysis for computerized surveillance. If the system can track different objects in an environment of multiple moving objects and reconstruct their trajectories, then there will be a variety of applications. This research is focused on reconstructing the trajectory of body movements in continuous stream of signals of a video for the purpose of further analysis and extracting information. Our method is based on the use of a moving object ontology to capture a more detailed information about the trajectory. The approach used in this article has not been explored much by the research community – see [1][2] for the use of structure motion description and initial estimations, [3][4] for the preset trajectory information in robotic control and [5][6] for interoperability of traditional trajectory information and generic sensors.

This research is part of the research program for Simulation-based Visual Analysis of Individual and Group Dynamic Behavior of the Cybersecurity Research Group of London Metropolitan University. The research group is interested in real-time video analytics with applicability to surveillance in security, disaster recovery and safety management, and customer insight. The ultimate goal of this research program is to construct an efficient framework for visual analytics in real time as shown in Fig. 1.

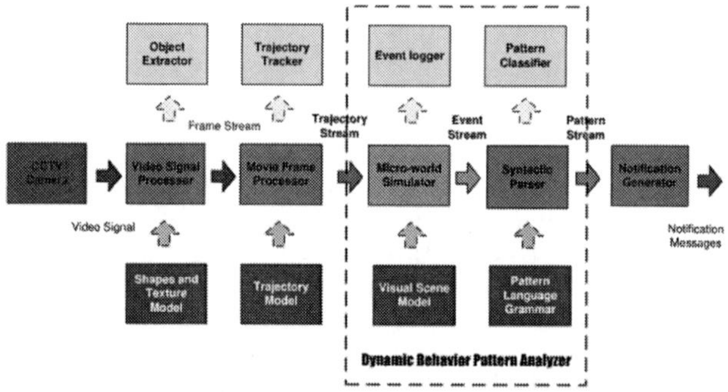

Figure 1. General workflow of the overall framework [8]

Moving object tracking in our approach is based on the object-centric representation of the position which forms a tube-like model of the spatial navigation and allows isolated manipulation of the video objects within the focus. This can be achieved through an incremental algorithm for processing the flow of information as illustrated in the Fig. 2.

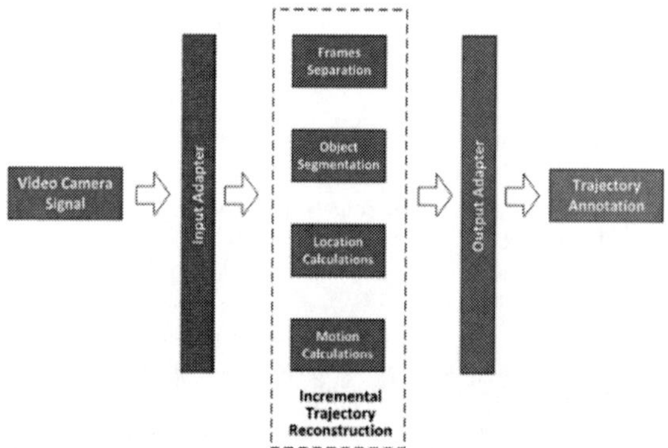

Figure 2. Incremental trajectory reconstruction

The moving human object in the video is modeled as a collection of spatiotemporal object volumes (object tubes). Key for reconstructing of the trajectory in this model is the estimation of the object positions and the navigation parameters of the object movements such as rotation, direction of movement and speed.

Reconstruction of moving object trajectories starts with extraction of the motion information from the video and representation of object trajectories in a 3D grid. Motion based on video representations have been used in other video navigation and annotation systems, but the focus of these systems is mainly on providing an in-scene direct moving object trajectory from the video. As expected, the reconstruction of the trajectory is based on analytical methods for connecting the spatial locations of the identified objects across the frames. This is pursued on the basis of incremental approximation of the spatial locations of the video frames using different computational techniques and approximations.

The rest of this paper is organized as follows; Section II describes the foundation of incremental reconstruction of trajectories. Section III describes the method of distance calculation. Section IV addresses the direction estimation. Section V goes into finer details about types of movements. Section VI explains about camera position. Section VII reports about the implementation of framework. The conclusions and references close the article.

II. Foundation for Incremental Reconstruction of the Trajectories

There are many ways to model the moving objects and they all have different values for the task of trajectory reconstruction. Researchers constantly search for better models in order to make the trajectories' reconstruction process more adequate as well as efficient, so that it can be used in real-time.

A. *Comparinsion of the basic geometric shapes*

Initially, our research started with a point-based model. After exploring the benefits and limitations of this model, we moved to a more adequate but more complex triangle shape-based model. Fig. 3 shows the trajectory reconstruction with the help of point based model:

Figure 3. Trajectory reconstructed using point based model

The moving object was tracked in the video and annotated graphically by dot shaped labels. Reconstructing of the trajectories with the point-based model is easy and needs less computational resources. The mathematical representation of the points requires only co-ordinates for the dots. It is relatively easy to extract this information from the video in order to reconstruct the trajectory of the moving object.

Point-based model is not appropriate for objects of different size. Also, it is not capable of representing the changes in the shape of object on a move. For instance, the bending and twisting of moving object cannot be represented in point-based model. Therefore, the authors decided to move to a prismatic shape model as it wraps up the whole volume of the physical object body. This is shown in Fig. 4.

Figure 4. Trajectory reconstructed using prismatic model

The prismatic model helps in estimating the size of the object. At the same time, there is a possibility that different prismatic shapes can represent the different parts of the moving object. The prismatic shapes can be combined to create bigger and even different shapes. For instance, a number of prismatic shapes when combined can form a sphere. This approach is widely adopted in computer games where the moving objects are wrapped up in an invisible "capsule".

This model is a step towards estimating the correct size of the moving object. But still it is not possible to cover the motion of the body parts of moving object, for instance, bending, and we are also unable to estimate the twisting of the moving object. To overcome these weaknesses, we obviously need to extend the moving object model through combining multiple shapes, but before that we need to consider its simpler counterpart, the spherical shape model, since it deals with rotations more naturally. Fig. 5 illustrates the trajectory based on spherical model.

Figure 5. Trajectory reconstructed using spherical model

B. *Choice of the composite model of the dynamic objects*

The starting point of the 3D reconstruction of the object movements using their 2D projections on the frames of a digital video signal is the choice of a suitable composite model. Different approximations are possible depending on the precision needed and the complexity of the recognition algorithms we can afford. For the purpose of the analysis at this stage of the research, we are using *seven spheres model* (see Figure 6). It is an optimal in the sense that it combines the simplicity of the spherical shape with the sophistication of the composite capsule.

The main parts of the body in this model are represented by separate spherical shapes with one extra sphere to cover the whole body. These six spheres allow tracking of the major type of motions – directed (like *forward*), rotational (like *turning left*), as well as relative to the body (like *bending* and *standing up*). This model can be presented schematically as shown in Fig. 6.

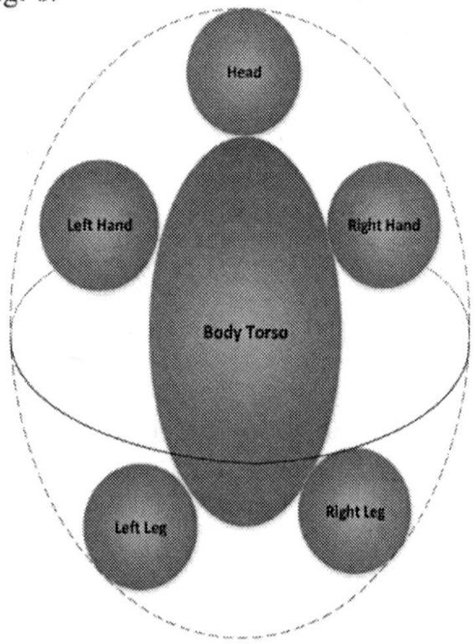

Figure 6. Seven spheres model

Other models are also possible but they all have different benefits and drawbacks from our point of view. The following table summarizes the comparison of some of the popular moving object models.

TABLE I. COMPARISION OF MOVING OBJECT MODELS

Moving object models	Model characteristics			
	Algorithmic Complexity	***Accuracy***	***Representing rotation***	***Amount of information***
Point-based model	Low	Low	No	Low
Spherical model	Low	Medium	No	Medium
Prismatic shape model	Medium	Medium	Yes	Medium
Seven spheres model	Medium	High	Yes	High
Six lines model	High	Highest	Yes	Highest

In future, we do not exclude the possibility to switch to more commonly accepted models such as the line-based similar to the body armature model endorsed by Microsoft in their game platform Kinect (see Fig. 7), but we believe that the seven spheres model is fully adequate for our purpose and has

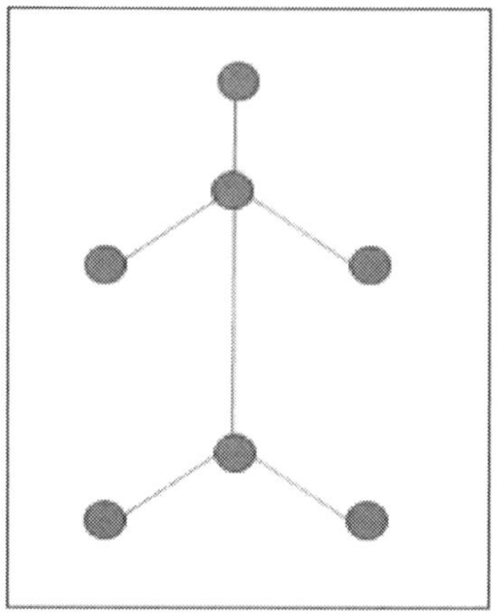

Figure 7. Representation of moving object using dots and lines

additional benefits from computational point of view, since the algorithms for extrapolating the volumes are more efficient.

III. CALCULATING DISTANCES

One of the challenges in this research is to find various distances within the 3D space based on the 2D projections on the video frames - between the camera and the moving object, between the front and the rear of an object etc. This is also known as *depth calculation*. There are some methods already available for this task, but they have their own limitations [8][9]. For instance, they need the camera focal length and other values for preliminary calibration, some methods require constant use of two cameras, etc.

To find a way to overcome this challenge, we have adopted a simple geometrical approach, which calculates the absolute 3D sizes based on their relative 2D projections; as all models used in this research have coordinates values about the moving object then these can be used to find the depth distance. Consider the configuration in Fig. 8:

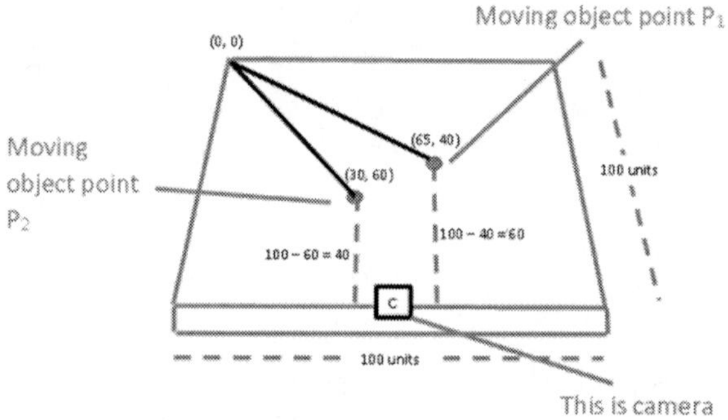

Figure 8. Moving object at point P1 and P2 at two different time instances with depth calculation

In this simple approach and in order to estimate absolute sizes, all what we need are the coordinates of the projections, assuming the position of the camera is fixed in the middle of the observable space. The advantage of this approach is in its simplicity and independence on any preparatory work although it may lead to more complex algorithms in the case of multiple cameras observing the same space.

IV. ESTIMATING DIRECTIONS

Two main directions need to be estimated for the purpose of the behavior analysis in video analytics – *navigation* (moving direction) and *line of sight* (viewing direction). The direction of movement is estimated entirely using analytical methods which use a simple geometry of space. As far as the viewing direction, we use a combinsation of statistical and analytical methods.

As a first approximation we assume that the viewing direction is the same as the moving direction, at a later stage the viewing direction will be corrected on the basis of the horizontal rotation of the sphere which represents the head. The following possible cases are forming the body of the algorithm for estimating the viewing direction:

- If the body is moving forward along a line then we will estimate the difference between the moving directions of the object over the time interval and if it is stable then the two directions are kept identical. If there is a change caused by rotation of the head, the viewing direction is estimated as the difference between the angle of side rotation and the moving direction.
- If the object is not moving, then the viewing direction is considered to be the difference between the angle of facing the camera and the angle of rotation of the head.
- If the head is rotating in both directions (i.e., oscillating horizontally) the amplitude of the oscillation is estimated to calculate the viewing direction as the middle point.

To implement the above algorithm two parameters have been introduced; the time instance head is turned into a different direction from the moving direction, and the amplitude of oscillation of the head around the viewing direction.

V. TYPE OF MOVEMENTS

In order to provide informative reconstruction of the trajectories, it is essential to track various possible spatial movements, the most important cases are as follows:

Continuous linear movement: The capsula is moving in a direction without rotation. This type of movement generates a simple trajectory.

Static object starts moving: In initial time instance, this static object does not move, however after a few ticks it changes the position. In initial time instance, there is no trajectory for this type of motion but after few time instances the trajectory appears.

Static object moves under the influence of another moving object: This type of motion is similar to the previous but in this case the object motion is caused by another moving object (*knock-down effect*); for instance, a walking person reaches a wall, picks a briefcase from the ground, drops it, etc. In this case the trajectory starts appearing after few time instances.

Moving object disappearing from the scene: At the beginning, the object has a trajectory, but at some point, this trajectory interrupts due to the objects navigating outside of the visual scope of the camera.

Object rotation: This rotation is either the whole moving object rotation or a rotation of some of its parts. This calculation is simpler with the spherical model.

VI. CHANGING THE CAMERA POSITION

All the explanations, figures, and descriptions included in this article are based on the use of two dimensional space as a projection of the three dimensional physical space.

A. *Standard Origin*

The origin of the two dimensional space is initially considered at the top left (or in three dimensional space, at the top left bottom) corner of the visual scope. The initial position of origin is illustrated in the Fig. 9 where spheres are used to represent the positions.

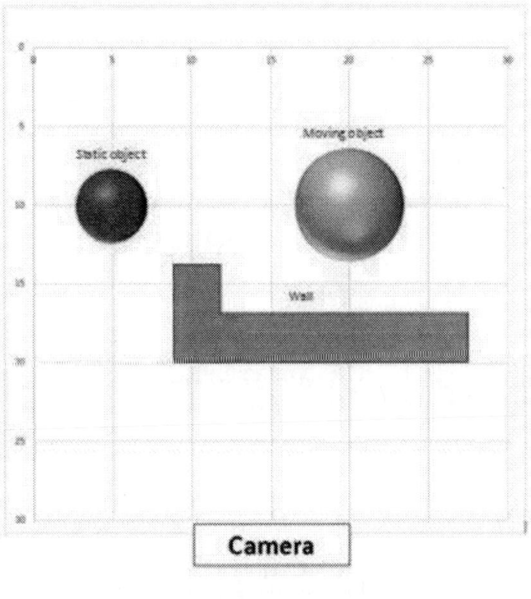

Figure 9. Normal space with origin at the top left corner

We assume that a camera is at the bottom center of the space. The calibration depends upon the space rather than upon the position of the camera so our choice is for convenience only. From the above figure the equation of the origin can be described as follows;

$$O = (x_{OO}, y_{OO}) \quad (1)$$

The position of a camera is represented below,

$$C = (x_{CO}, y_{CO}) \quad (2)$$

While the position of the sphere is expressed as;

$$S = (x_{SO}, y_{SO}) \quad (3)$$

The vector from the camera to the sphere can be described as;

$$\overrightarrow{CS} = \vec{C} - \vec{S} \quad (4)$$

$$\overrightarrow{CS} = (x_{SO} - x_{cO}, y_{sO} - y_{cO}) \quad (5)$$

The length of the vector can be given as;

$$|\overrightarrow{CS}| = \sqrt{(x_{SO} - x_{cO})^2 + (y_{sO} - y_{cO})^2} \quad (6)$$

B. Shifting the origin at the camera location

To make the whole calculation and explanation simpler, we can move the origin of the space to the position of the camera. This is shown in Fig. 10 where red rectangles denote the updated calibrations.

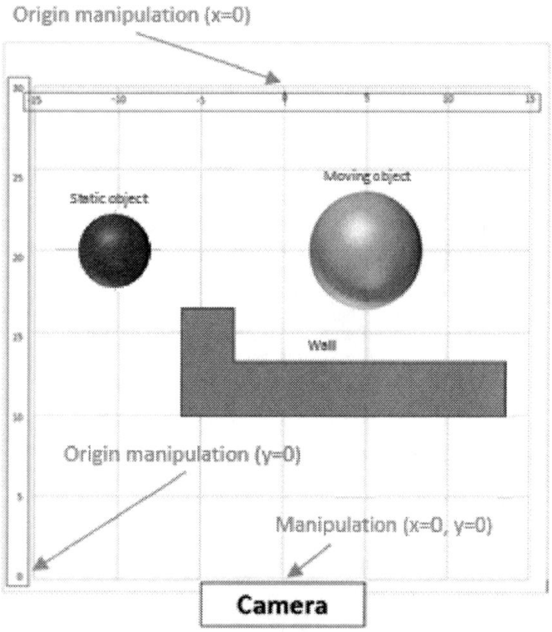

Figure 10. Modified space with the origin at the camera location

The new origin position can be rewritten as below:

$$O' = (x_{oo} + a, y_{oo} + b) \quad (7)$$

where a is the displacement value of the origin along X-Axis, while b is the displacement value of the origin along Y-Axis.

Due to the above origin displacement, now the camera position is the same as the origin;

$$C' = (x_{oo} + a, y_{oo} + b) \quad (8)$$

The position of the sphere with respect to the new origin is;

$$S' = (x_{s0} - a, y_{s0} - b) \quad (9)$$

By default, the values a and b should be subtracted from the original value of the sphere. However, if origin displacement involves crossing of the sphere position then the final value should be multiplied by -1. In this case the new vector between a camera and a sphere can be given as below;

$$\overrightarrow{C'S'} = \overrightarrow{C'} - \overrightarrow{S'} \quad (10)$$

$$\overrightarrow{C'S'} = ((x_{s0} - a) - (x_{oo} + a), (y_{s0} - b) - (y_{oo} + b)) \quad (11)$$

Then, the distance between the camera and the sphere is;

$$\overrightarrow{C'S'} = \sqrt{((x_{s0} - a) - (x_{oo} + a))^2 + ((y_{s0} - b) - (y_{oo} + b))^2} \quad (12)$$

All above calculations are relatively simple and can be implemented efficiently which allows the algorithms to be executed in real-time without much difficulties.

VII. IMPLEMENTATION OF THE FRAMEWORK

The trajectory reconstruction module of the video analytics framework does the actual processing of the video frames using **OpenCV** open source engine [10]. The module supports the following main operations;

- High-level GUI and Media I/O
- Image processing of the video frames
- Geometric transformations
- Structural analysis and shape approximation

The module operates in real-time using recurrent algorithms based on the model described in the paper. It includes several components which are introduced below;

A. Selection of video frames for processing

Every video data consist of video frames which are 2D graphical objects. These frames are combined in the time sequence to form a video by the digital devices as shown in Fig. 11.

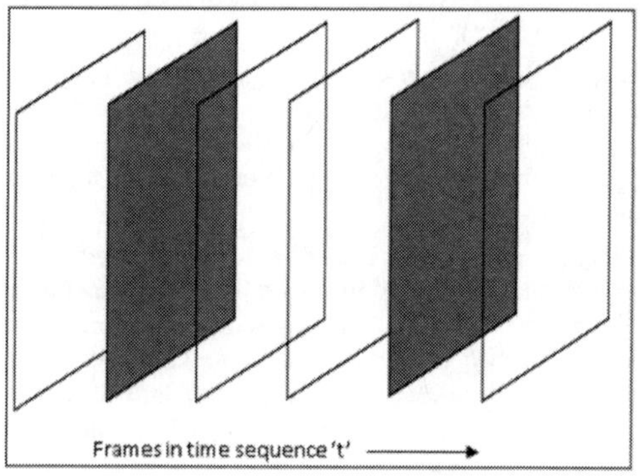

Figure 11. Sequence of frames

Typically, most of the CCTV and HDTV surveillance cameras produce frames at a rate which does not exceed thirty frames per second. The above figure illustrates the flow of frames in a video movie.

Most of the video processing frameworks do not process each and every frame of video data. Some of the frames presented in the above picture are shown in white color and few more are shown in gray color because we assume that we are processing only the frames in grey after skipping few frames in white. The criteria for choosing which frames to process depends on the complexity of the algorithms and the frame content.

B. Moving objects segmentation

This component of the trajectory reconstruction module performs operations on all selected frames to identify and approximate the contour of the objects within the frame (Fig. 12).

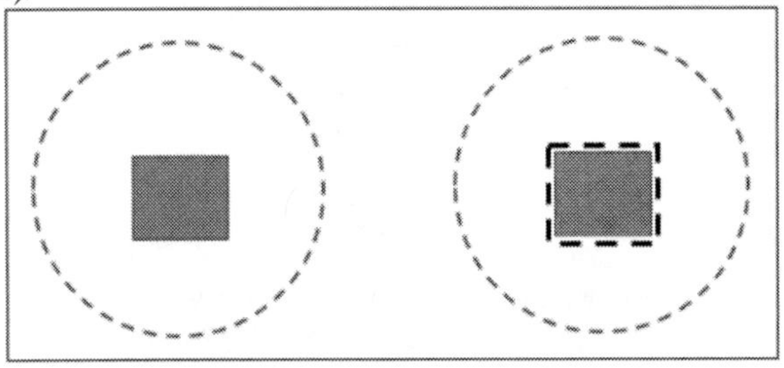

Figure 12. Moving object and sequences of points around the moving object shaping its projection on the frame

The segmentation component first converts the frame into binary format and then performs processing of the pixels to find the approximate contour of the moving object.

C. Computing moving objects displacement

Displacement component keeps track of the moving object identified by the segmentation component of the module. It calculates the displacement of the moving objects in each processed frame which is needed for subsequent trajectory reconstruction.

D. Reconstructing the moving objects trajectory

The reconstructed trajectory data is calculated on the basis of the information about object location, their descriptors and the values of displacement. It is a continuous stream of information calculated recurrently and generated as an output of the module for further analysis.

VIII. CONCLUSION

This paper presents an efficient model-driven approach to moving object trajectory reconstruction which can be used for real-time video analytics. Our approach has a number of advantages compared to Microsoft Kinect model commonly endorsed in computer games industry [11][12]. First, the trajectory data can be reconstructed using less information because of the simpler geometry which lowers the requirements for preliminary visual image processing. Secondly, the reconstruction of the trajectory is more efficient because of the simpler approximation, which makes this approach preferable for real-time systems. Thirdly, the overall algorithms of moving object trajectory reconstruction are far simpler than the other algorithms reviewed in the literature and the software becomes more compact, which allows an easy embedding in other software for visual analytics.

Our immediate plans, after finalizing the trajectory reconstruction module, is to implement an extension for estimating the viewing direction, which is needed for further analysis of the dynamic behavior patterns in areas such as customer insight. Next, we are planning to enhance our model through combining features of the seven spheres model used here with the six lines model of Kinect in order to be able to analyze gestures as well.

REFERENCES

[1] D. Walther, U. Rutishauser, and C. Koch, "On the usefulness of attention for object recognition", second international workshop on attention and performance in computational vision (WAPCV '04), pp. 96–103, Conference: Prague, Czech Republic, 2004.

[2] S. Alpert, M. Galun, and A. Brandt, Image Segmentation by Probabilistic Bottom-Up Aggregation and Cue Integration, IEEE transactions on pattern analysis and machine intelligence, pp. 315 – 319, 2012

[3] O. Gerovich, P. Marayong, and A. M. Okamura, "The effect of visual and haptic feedback on computer-assisted needle insertion," Journal of Computer Aided Surgery, pp. 243-249, 2004

[4] R. Alterovitz and K. Goldberg, "Motion Planning in Medicine: Optimization and Simulation Algorithms for Image-Guided Procedures," Springer-Verlag, Berlin Heidelberg, 2008.

[5] A. M. Okamura, C. Simone, and M. D. O'Leary, "Force modeling for needle insertion into soft tissue," IEEE Trans. Biomed. Eng., vol. 51, no. 10, pp. 1707-1716, Oct. 2004.

[6] L. Zhang, X. Wen, W. Zheng, and B. Wang , "An Algorithm for Moving Semantic Objects Trajectories Detection in Video". Proc. of IEEE International Conference on Information Theory and Information Security (ICITIS), pp. 34-27, 2010

[7] A. Boulmakoul, L. Karim, A. Elbouziri, and A. Lbath, "A System Architecture for Heterogeneous Moving-Object Trajectory Metamodel Using Generic Sensors: Tracking Airport Security Case Study", IEEE Systems Journal, vol. 9, pp. 28-291, March 2015

[8] P. Gasiorowski, V. Vassilev and K. Ouazzane, "Simulation-based Visual Analysis of Individual and Group Dynamic Behavior". In: Proc. 20th International Conference on Image Processing, Computer Vision, & Pattern Recognition (IPCV'16), pp. 303-309, 25-28 July, 2016, Las Vegas, USA.

[9] M. Salmistraro, M. Zamarin, L. Raket and S. Forchhammer, "Distributed multi-hypothesis coding of depth maps using texture motion information and optical flow", IEEE International Conference on Acoustics, Speech and Signal Processing, conference: Vancouver, BC, pp. 1685 - 1689, May 2013.

[10] M. Kim, N, Ling and L. Song, "Fast single depth intra mode decision for depth map coding in 3D-HEVC", IEEE International Conference on Multimedia & Expo Workshops (ICMEW), pp. 1-6, June 2015.

[11] OpenCV library explanation and source https://sourceforge.net/projects/opencvlibrary/files/opencv-win/2.4.13/opencv-2.4.13.exe/download [Last accessed: 20-06-2016]

[12] Developing with Kinect for Windows https://developer.microsoft.com/en-us/windows/kinect/develop [Last accessed: 20-06-2016]

A Fast Audiovisual Attention Model for Human Detection and Localization on a Companion Robot

Rémi Ratajczak, Denis Pellerin, Quentin Labourey
CNRS, GIPSA-Lab
Univ. Grenoble Alpes
F-38000 Grenoble, France
email: remi.ratajczak@gmail.com
email: denis.pellerin@gipsa-lab.grenoble-inp.fr
email: quentin.labourey@gipsa-lab.grenoble-inp.fr

Catherine Garbay
CNRS, LIG
Univ. Grenoble Alpes
F-38000 Grenoble, France
email: catherine.garbay@imag.fr

***Abstract*—This paper describes a fast audiovisual attention model applied to human detection and localization on a companion robot. Its originality lies in combining static and dynamic modalities over two analysis paths in order to guide the robot's gaze towards the most probable human beings' locations based on the concept of saliency. Visual, depth and audio data are acquired using a RGB-D camera and two horizontal microphones. Adapted state-of-the-art methods are used to extract relevant information and fuse them together via two dimensional gaussian representations. The obtained saliency map represents human positions as the most salient areas. Experiments have shown that the proposed model can provide a mean F-measure of 66 percent with a mean precision of 77 percent for human localization using bounding box areas on 10 manually annotated videos. The corresponding algorithm is able to process 70 frames per second on the robot.**

Keywords-audiovisual attention; saliency; RGB-D; human localization; companion robot.

I. INTRODUCTION

With the rapid advances in robotics, companion robots will tend to be more and more integrated in the human daily life [12]. These robots have the particularity to be both sociable, mobile and destined to evolve in an indoor domestic environment. One of the main requirement for them is to be able to quickly analyze their surrounding in order to interact with humans. That is why it is necessary to prioritize the perception, detection and localization of humans. They also need to behave as natural as possible in order to become acceptable presences for the humans [12].

To reach these requirements, cognitive based audiovisual attention mechanisms are a possibility that has been investigated in this work. Their related concepts can indeed provide the robot with the natural idea that it should give more attention to some positions than others.

A fast multimodal attention model for human detection and localization on a companion robot has thus been conceptualized and developed.

This model is distinctive from state-of-the-art methods presented in Section II due to both its application on a robot that can travel between different places during time, and to its architecture that combines visual, depth and audio data through two independent static and dynamic analysis paths. Moreover, since the robot and the humans can both move, the robot will not ever be in a situation where a specific characteristic of a human (face, leg, etc.) would be detectable. And since the detectors associated with these characteristics may sometimes fail, it has been decided not to use them in the proposed model in order to avoid false detections. This model may thus be considered as a bottom-up external information guided model.

Figure 1. Photography of the robot Qbo Pro Evo without the Asus Xtion Pro Live RGB-D Camera.

It has been realized using the open source robot Qbo Pro Evo (Fig. 1) produced by TheCorpora©. Qbo's height is of 456 millimeters. It integrates an Intel i3-2120T 2.6 gigahertz processor and 4 gigabytes of random access memory. This hardware is conducted by a Linux Mint 17.1 operating system that has been enhanced with the Indigo's version of the Robotic Operating System (ROS). It embeds an Asus Xtion Pro Live RGB-D camera at the top of its head. This camera can stream depth and color images with a resolution of 640 by 480 pixels at 30 frames per second (FPS). It also provides two stereo microphones with a gap of 147.5 millimeters between them. Thanks to this system, the proposed model is able to analyze multimodal data as soon as they arrive.

The rest of this paper is organized as follows. Section II describes state-of-the-art ideas about audiovisual attention and its applications to robotics. Section III describes the proposed model in details. Section IV presents the dataset that has been used and the results of the evaluation. Section V concludes this study and presents future work perspectives related to the proposed model.

II. Previous Work

This section presents previous work related to the proposed model.

A. Audiovisual attention

Audiovisual attention is a fast human cognitive process that aims to guide human interest through the most salient (i.e., remarkable) areas [7]. This process has been widely studied during the past three decades in neurosciences, psychology and computer sciences. This section focuses on the computational models developed using computer sciences methods.

Their goal is to represent the saliency level of different sources on a grayscale image called saliency map. On this map, the more salient an element is, the higher its intensity is [7]. Most attention models are referred as saliency models.

As described in [2], a huge number of saliency models have been implemented during time. Their efficiencies have been evaluated on different benchmarks using neurosciences ground truth results [3].

Anyway, these benchmarks are mostly available for the models designed for static two dimensional images only. They are not suitable to evaluate a multimodal or a dynamical model. This may be explained by the fact that most of state-of-the-art work are only based on static visual data ("single input image" [3]). These models have the particularity to give out salient regions independently of the content of the scene. This means that they may detect elements that do not correspond to a given target. In order to bias the results obtained with those classical models, some works have however incorporated other modalities, such as depth, motion, or sound.

Reference [5] demonstrated the utility to use a depth bias over two dimensional visual saliency results in order to increase their efficiency on ground truth evaluations obtained through eye-tracking processes. The authors notably concluded that humans are more attentive to close elements.

Reference [9] proposed to use motion detection on video images in order to localize areas that are moving and to combine them with a 2D static saliency model. The idea behind this is that the human gaze may be more attracted by moving objects than static objects. The authors proposed to drastically increase the saliency of moving objects.

Reference [4] has shown that adding sound analysis to visual cues may help to increase the saliency of a talking human for dynamic conversational purposes. Reference [10] used a visual additive two dimensional Gaussian bias centered on a horizontal sound localized position to improve the detection of a target in a complex visual environment.

B. Applications in robotics

Applications of the attention's concepts in the field of robotics are still uncommon but are gaining more and more importance in the design of methods for robots' perception.

Reference [11] proposed to combine a static visual attention model with a two dimensional sound localization to guide the gaze of a static humanoid robot thanks to the Head Related Transfer Function (HRTF) transform. This transform is effective to localize a sound in a human manner. However, it requires precisely designed humanoid ears covering the microphones, making the results of the HRTF difficult to reproduce with a standard robot such as Qbo.

Reference [12] used a multimodal approach to control the emotions of a sitting conversational humanoid robot according to the most interesting face of the human being. The authors used color, depth and sound data. In their method, they considered that the human faces will always be present in the scene. They used specific methods for human characterization such as emotion and head pose recognition. Their camera was detached of the robot and connected to an external computer. They did not consider algorithm speed issues.

III. Proposed Model

This section presents a novel approach for human detection and localization using audiovisual attention concepts on a companion robot. It has been inspired by the previously described independent literature results that have rarely been combined all together. The corresponding model thus combines multiple state-of-the-art ideas and methods in an all-in-one modular model represented on Fig. 2. It extracts independent static and dynamic features using visual, depth, and sound data. These features are then fused together in order to increase the saliency of the areas that may correspond the most to a human being.

In order to achieve this goal, the proposed model has been designed considering real domestic conditions through the following hypotheses: hypothesis (1) the robot will sometimes not be in presence of a human being, hypothesis (2) the robot may move over time, and will thus see different places with different points of view, hypothesis (3) a human being is a multimodal entity that can move and emit sound that the robot should be attentive to, hypothesis (4) the robot should be more attentive to close elements in order to avoid background salient elements detection, and hypothesis (5) the model has to be fast in order to eventually enable other processes to run at the same time on the robot. Its development was made considering the robot stationary while analyzing a scene. The mobility constraint has been considered through hypothesis (2).

A. Processing architecture of the model

As shown on Fig. 2, the proposed model has been decomposed in five steps and two independent static and dynamic analysis paths. It combines static visual 2D saliency with depth, motion and sound biases as referred in Section II.A. These modalities have been chosen according to the hypothesis (3) made in Section III. From a computational point of view, the model has been first developed using Matlab toolboxes before it was implemented on the robot using the C++ language through the ROS packages structure and the open source libraries OpenNI and OpenCV.

In the following sections, the proposed model is going to be presented step by step, from static to dynamic modalities and from visual to audio cues.

B. Step 1 – Data retrieval

This step's goal is to get the data from the sensors.

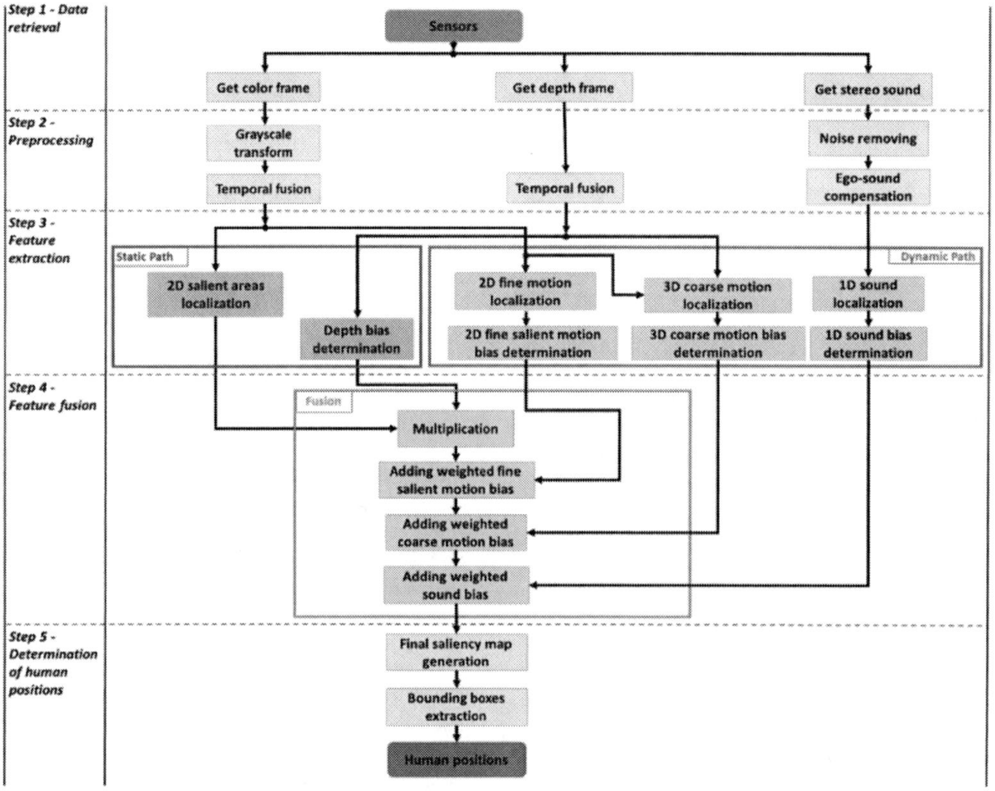

Figure 2. Flow chart of the proposed model.

As explained in Section I, color and depth images are both acquired at a speed of 30 FPS with a resolution of 640 by 480 pixels thanks to the RGB-D camera.

Stereo sound signals are discretized using a sample frequency of 44.1 kilohertz and bufferized in a one dimensional array.

C. Step 2 – Preprocessing

This step aims to reduce observation noises and computational time using simple but efficient operations. The following observations about the data have been made during this study:

- Color channels are not used in Step 3.
- Illumination variations generate noise on both color and depth images.
- Randomly located "holes" can be observed on depth images (i.e., not out of range areas that are considered as if they were out of range).
- Sound signals show an inconstant amplitude offset coming from the functionning robot's system ego-sound.

The following operations have been realized. Their results are shown on Fig. 3.

First, the last retrieved color image is converted in grayscale, dividing by three times its computational cost.

Second, in order to improve the robustness of the images to noisy variations during time, a simple but efficient approach, driven by empirical considerations, has been chosen. It consists in blending the current image with the previous blended image. The resulting image is named reference image. Equation (1) describes this temporal fusion. This method has the advantage to take care of the hypothesis (2) made in section III because it does not consider explicit background information for illumination noise removing.

$$I_{ref}(t) = \propto \times I(t) + (1-\propto) \times I(t-1) \qquad (1)$$

In (1), α represents a parameter that can increase or decrease the importance of the previous images over time. The lower α is, the higher their importance is. Therefore, having a low α is important to consequently reduce noise variations over time, but it also gives less importance to the current image and tends to generate a less precisely localized motion. In the proposed model, α has been set to 0.8 for color (grayscaled) images and to 0.2 for depth images in order to smooth the depth holes while not having a high incident on the motion localization described in Sections III.D.3 and III.D.4.

Third, the noise from sound data is filtered with a low-pass 6th order Butterworth filter using a cut off frequency of

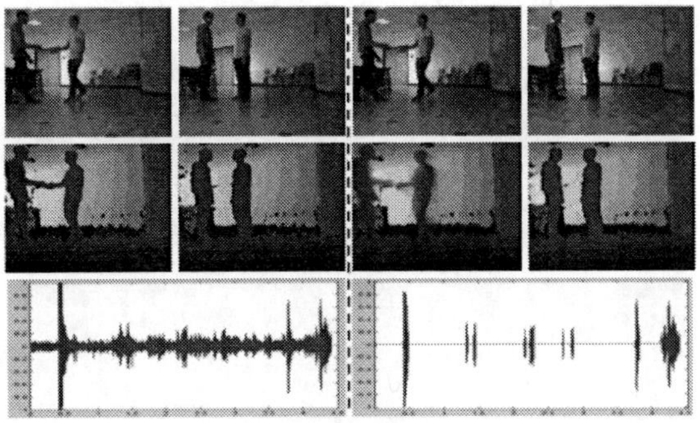

Figure 3. Example of data as obtained before (left) and after (right) the pre-process step. (a) color images; (b) depth images; (c) sound.

4 kilohertz designed on Matlab. It is then thresholded according to the intensity of its energy in order to avoid false detections coming from the ego-sound of the robot. The threshold used has been determined by analyzing energy values on 33 milliseconds records with and without external sound.

D. Step 3 – Feature extraction

This step represents the multiple processes that are applied to extract the interesting features used in the fusion step. It has been separated in two paths. The static path includes modalities that will always be detected. The dynamic path includes modalities that may be present at instant "t" but may be absent at instant "t+1". After each process of a same step, resulting images are normalized. The results are shown on Fig 4.

1) 2D salient areas localization: This process consists in applying a visual static saliency model to the previously grayscaled reference image. Like in [1], the model of [6] has been choosen for its efficency and its rapidity. Its principle is based on the spectral residual concept. The idea behind this is that salient areas on natural images (i.e., not artificial) may be considered as the less redundant ones. The method of [6] consists in applying a fast discrete two dimensional Fourier transform on a grayscale image of size 64 by 64 pixels. A logarithmic transform and a 3 by 3 mean filter are then applied to the amplitude spectrum of this image. The spectral residual spectrum is obtained via the substraction of the mean logarithmic representation with the original amplitude spectrum. The inverse fast discrete 2D Fourier transform is then used with the spectral residual spectrum instead of the amplitude spectrum. The resulting image is filtered with a 7 by 7 gaussian filter in order to obtain a 2D saliency map representing gaussian salient areas.

2) Depth bias determination: The goal of this process is to make the depth reference image represent closest values with the highest intensities in order to use the depth bias concept of [5] in the fusion step. It provides the robot with a more human-like perception model. It also helps to consider the hypothesis (4) described in Section III. First, the image is subsampled to a resolution of 64 by 64 pixels in order to be spatially equivalent to the saliency map. Its intensity values are then inversed. Values that are out of the sensor's range are set to zero in order to represent the absence of information. Finally, a closing operator with 3 by 3 rectangular structuring element is applied in order to remove the small detected holes.

3) 2D fine motion localization and fine salient motion bias determination: These processes aim to detect motion between consecutive reference images and to represent the saliency levels of the moving areas. This motion is considered as fine because it is detected on full resolution images. It is thus considered as able to capture motion having both small and high amplitudes. Since this process needs to be fast, a well known mean of the absolute difference operation is used via (2). The mean filter helps to remove false and small detected moving areas. Its size is of N by N pixels. N is equal to 7 in this model.

$$I_{diff}(x,y,t) = \frac{1}{N^2} \sum_{-\frac{N-1}{2}}^{\frac{N-1}{2}} | I(x+i,y+j,t) - I(x+i,y+j,t-1) | \quad (2)$$

The process described in Section III.D.1. is then applied on the resulting difference image. The obtained result represents the detected motion through a salient gaussian areas representation: the 2D fine salient motion bias.

4) 3D coarse motion localization and coarse motion bias determination: These processes aim to detect motion between consecutive reference images that have been subsampled to a resolution of 64 by 64 pixels. It has been supposed to be only able to detect motions having a high enough amplitude. This motion is thus considered only if a fine motion as been detected. Moreover, since we have access to both depth and color (grayscaled) images, the coarse motion is detected on both in order to provide a more robust motion localization with the idea of a three dimensionnal motion. First, (2) is applied on the subsampled reference images. Second, an additive mean of the two difference images is realized in order to combine both motion representations. The result is binarized keeping only pixels with an intensity higher than 60% of the maximal possible value. The binarized areas are named blobs. Only blobs containing at least 40 pixels are considered as true moving areas. Their centroids are found and convoluted with a vertical gaussian whose size depends of the mean depth value obtained on a 3 by 3 area around the centroids. This representation is the 3D coarse motion bias.

5) 1D sound localization and sound bias determination: The sound is localized on the horizontal dimension using the cross correlation and the Interaural Time Difference (ITD) of [8]. First, a sound buffer of 33 milliseconds is retrieved from the two microphones. The size of this buffer corresponds to the required time in order to get an image with the camera. A cross correlation between left and right sound components is applied using a moving window of 20 samples. The ITD is then determined. It gives the angle position of the detected sound in the robot coordinates. This angle is converted in the 64 by 64 image pixels coordinates and a vertical gaussian is set at the sound location according to [10]. This is the 1D sound bias.

E. Step 4 – Feature fusion

This step aims to obtain the final saliency map by successively combining the various detected features from step 3 according to the hypotheses developed in Section III.

First, saliency and depth bias are combined through an element by element multiplication. This operation has been chosen in order to only impact the already salient areas. Then, the non-zero dynamic biases are successively added to the result. These operations are weighted additions in order to modify the relative saliency levels between the areas of the previously obtained image. The weights for fine motion, coarse motion and sound biases are respectively 60%, 60% and 30% in order to give a lot of importance to motions. Since experiments have shown that sound cannot be localized as precisely as visual features and as it is added after the motions, its weight is lower than motions' ones.

F. Step 5 – Determination of human positions

Human positions are retrieved using bounding boxes generated from the final saliency map. Bounding boxes are localized over the areas with a final saliency intensity of at least 50% of the maximal possible intensity in order to eliminate outliers without advantaging precision nor recall.

In order to define whether a detected bounding box should be considered as a human position, the correlation between a human being presence and the detected dynamic modalities has been learned. These modalities are represented by the dynamic biases and are the only available information sources that can help to make a *decision* about the eventual detection of a human being. The dataset described in Section IV has been used. The results are shown on Tab. 1. True positives (TP) correspond to a modality detection while a human is present, and false positives (FP) correspond to a detection when no human is present. True negatives (TN) and false negatives (FN) are also represented. The total detected (TD) values indicate when a modality has been detected over all the images.

Since all the false positive rates are low, it has been decided to use a simple binary *decision* for this model: if at least a fine motion or a sound has been detected, then it means that a human has been detected (i.e., is present).

TABLE I. CORRELATIONS BETWEEN DETECTED MODALITIES AND A HUMAN BEING PRESENCE (34 VIDEOS, 4 SOUND RECORDS).

	Fine Motion (%)	Coarse Motion (%)	Sound (%)
TD	82.7	42.5	2.2
TP	80	42.4	2.2
FP	2.7	0.1	0
TN	11.5	14.0	24.0
FN	5.8	43.5	73.8

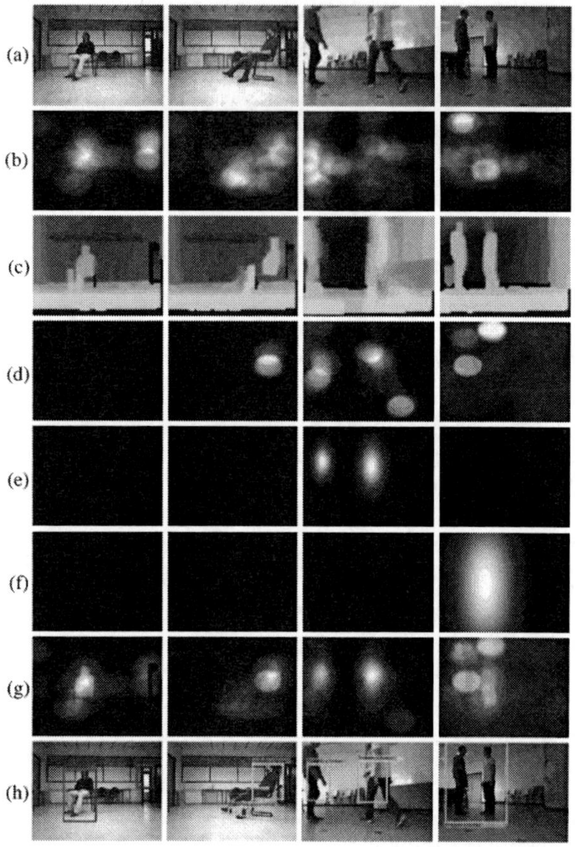

Figure 4. Example of results obtained by the model. Black images mean no information. (a) color (grayscaled) reference image; (b) salient areas; (c) depth bias; (d) fine motion bias; (e) coarse motion bias; (f) sound bias; (g) final saliency map; (h) bounding boxes. Red boxes indicate a lack of information for human detection, green boxes indicate probable human areas.

At this step, detected bounding boxes may be classified using their mean saliency values in order to determine which area is the most interesting. This operation may be useful in order to keep only one area to guide the robot's gaze towards the most interesting position.

IV. Evaluation of the Results

The results obtained by the proposed model have been evaluated on a dataset that has been acquired with the robot in two different rooms. It is made of 34 videos with durations between 7 and 20 seconds for a total of 10312 images. Only 4 videos also include sound data. At least one human is present on a part of each video. This human may be moving, sitting, standing or talking at any distance from the robot, but he is not necessarily always in the field of vision of the camera. The videos have been manually annotated with the frame ranges on which humans are present. For 10 of these videos (2 with sound), annotations also include the bounding box locations (ground truth) corresponding to the human 2D positions.

TABLE II. MEAN PRECISION, RECALL AND F-MEASURE WITH BOUNDING BOXES AFTER EACH FUSION (+). DETAILS FOR 2 VIDEOS WITH SOUND (W/+-) ARE PROVIDED. HIGHEST VALUES ARE IN GREEN, SECOND HIGHEST VALUES ARE IN BLUE. *DECISION* KEEPS ONLY BONDING BOXES WHEN HUMANS SHOULD HAVE BEEN DETECTED.

	Precision (%)		Recall (%)		F-measure (%)	
Decision?	yes	no	yes	no	yes	no
Saliency	28	22	35	29	32	26
+ Depth	44	35	42	35	43	35
+ Fine Motion	72	56	60	50	66	53
+ Coarse Motion	77	60	55	46	66	53
w/- Sound	79	73	44	39	57	51
w/+ Sound	76	70	49	44	59	54

First, the resulting bounding box locations from step 5 have been compared with the ground truth using Matlab. The comparison method was to determine the precision, the recall and the F-measure between the bounding box areas obtained by the model and the ground truth. It has been determined that the model is able to generate a mean F-measure of 66% with a precision of 77% for human localization. The detailed results are shown on Tab. 2.

The following are a detailed explanation of these results. First, depth helps to increase both the recall and the precision of the human localization generated by the saliency. This corresponds to the fact that when humans are close to the robot, it is difficult to define very salient areas because humans are recovering a large amount of the image, it gives them an important spatial redundancy and induces difficulties for the method of [6]. Second, the hypotheses that have been made about the dynamic data are confirmed: they greatly improve the human localization. It is interesting to observe that the coarse motion bias does not improve the F-measure but the precision, and that the sound bias improves both the recall and the F-measure. Moreover, these results do not support the fact that humans may be detected even in the absence of dynamic data thanks to saliency. This means that one should use a specific detector on the detected areas in order to characterize them. In that case, the specific detector would not be used as an input of the model like in [12], but like a final recognition step.

Third, since a fast model was desired through the hypothesis (5) detailed in Section III, the computational time of the proposed model has been evaluated at different instants in time after the algorithm has been adapted in C++. The robot is able to process incoming flow at a mean speed of 70 FPS, which is twice more than required to process every frame using the Asus Xtion Pro Live RGB-D camera.

V. CONCLUSION AND FUTURE WORK

In this paper, an original approach to detect and localize human beings using audiovisual attention's concepts on an indoor companion robot has been presented. It is able to detect and localize humans at 70 FPS with a mean F-measure of 66% and a precision of 77% using bounding boxes on a stationary robot.

Since the proposed model uses motion and sound localization, future work will focus on studying the effect of ego motion compensation on this model using visual and non-visual odometry state-of-the-art methods. Adding a supplementary step in order to characterize detected areas while no dynamic data is available will also be studied. The adaptation of the proposed model to other depth sensors will be considered in order to make it suitable for an outdoor use.

AKNOWLEDGEMENT

This work has been partially supported by the LabEx PERSYVAL-lab (ANR-11-LABX-0025-01) funded by the French program Investissement d'avenir.

REFERENCES

[1] S. Anwar, Q. Zhao, S. I. Khan, F. Manzoor, and N. Qadeer, "Spectral saliency model for an appearance only SLAM in an indoor environment," 11th International Bhurban Conference on Applied Sciences & Technology (IBCAST) Islamabad, Pakistan, Islamabad, pp. 118-125, Jan. 2014.

[2] A. Borji and L. Itti, "State-of-the-Art in Visual Attention Modeling," IEEE Trans. Pattern Analysis and Machine Intelligence vol. 35, no. 1, pp. 185-206, Jan. 2013.

[3] A. Borji, M. M. Cheng, H. Jiang, and J. Li, "Salient Object Detection: A Benchmark," in IEEE Transactions on Image Processing, vol. 24, no. 12, pp. 5706-5722, Dec. 2015.

[4] A. Coutrot and N. Guyader, "How saliency, faces, and sound influence gaze in dynamic social scenes," Journal of Vision, vol. 14, no. 8, pp. 1–17, 2014.

[5] J. Gautier and O. Le Meur, "A time-dependent saliency model combining center and depth biases for 2D and 3D viewing conditions," Cognitive Computation, Springer, 4 (2), pp.141-156, 2012.

[6] X. Hou and L. Zhang, "Saliency Detection: A Spectral Residual Approach," Proc. IEEE Conf. Computer Vision and Pattern Recognition, pp. 1-8, 2007.

[7] L. Itti, C. Koch, and E. Niebur, "A Model of Saliency-Based Visual Attention for Rapid Scene Analysis," IEEE Trans. Pattern Analysis and Machine Intelligence, vol. 20, no. 11, pp. 1254-1259, Nov. 1998.

[8] Q. Labourey, O. Aycard, D. Pellerin, and M. Rombaut, "Audiovisual data fusion for successive speakers tracking," Computer Vision Theory and Applications (VISAPP), International Conference on, Lisbon, Portugal, pp. 696-701, 2014.

[9] S. Marat, T. Ho-Phuoc, L. Granjon, N. Guyader, D. Pellerin, and A. Guérin-Dugué, "Modeling Spatio-Temporal Saliency to Predict Gaze Direction for Short Videos," Int. J. Computer Vision, vol. 82, pp. 231-243, 2009.

[10] S. Ramenahalli et al., "Audio-visual saliency map: Overview, basic models and hardware implementation," Information Sciences and Systems (CISS), 47th Annual Conference on, Baltimore, MD, pp. 1-6, 2013.

[11] J. Ruesch et al., "Multimodal Saliency-Based Bottom-Up Attention, A Framework for the Humanoid Robot iCub," IEEE International Conference on Robotics and Automation, Pasadena, pp. 962-967, 2008.

[12] A. Zaraki, D. Mazzei, M. Giuliani, and D. De Rossi, "Designing and Evaluating a Social Gaze-Control System for a Humanoid Robot," IEEE Transactions on Human-Machine Systems, vol. 44, no. 2, pp. 157–168, 2014.

A Method of Object Identification Based on Sea Image Processing

Jing Zhang
College of Computer Science and Technologyzation
Harbin Engineering University
Harbin, Heilongjiang, China
e-mail: zhangjing@hrbeu. edu. cn

Shaoyan Rao
College of Computer Science and Technologyzation
Harbin Engineering University
Harbin, Heilongjiang, China
e-mail: raoshaoyan@hrbeu. edu. cn

Tianchi Zhang
College of Computer Science and Technology,
Harbin Engineering University,
Harbin, Heilongjiang, China
e-mail: zhangtianchi@hrbeu. edu. cn

Abstract—**Currently, the technological evolution has led to the birth of the image processing discipline which processes and analyzes images in different fields including marine image processing. Identifying a dolphin from a picture which has sea feature is difficult because the background of the picture is complex and has some similarities with the target. For this reason, we make a thorough research on the target segmentation and the existing identification algorithms used to solve this problem. In this paper, we will present a new segmentation algorithm based on clustering threshold in the RGB color space to process dolphin images. We will combine it with the SIFT algorithm for image post-processing feature extraction. Then we will present how to build a dolphin growth model to identify a dolphin.**

Keywords—dolphin identification; sea image processing; target image segmentation; growth model; SIFT feature matching algorithm

I. INTRODUCTION

In digital image processing, it is desired that the machine recognition is capable of recognizing the object effectively from the complicated image and make a judgment, same as the human eye discriminates. Therefore, research and application of image segmentation technology and image recognition technology are very significant. Now, image recognition technology has been applied in more and more fields, such as face recognition, medical image processing and ocean image processing. We are interested in the application of the image recognition technology in recognizing dolphins.

Dolphins are some of the world's animals that are at risk of extinction. When wild dolphins' conservation experts study the wild dolphin colonies, they often estimate the age of dolphins by the artificial method. The method is that they need to compare the photographs one by one to estimate the age and distinguish individual dolphins according to the characteristics of the surface of dolphins. For experienced maritime workers, the correct rate of recognition of dolphin is relatively high. However, in order to distinguish the dolphins accurately, young marine workers need to take a lot of time to learn. The artificial recognition method has a big workload and high error rate. Therefore, we need to explore a new method of image recognition to solve these problems.

Ma Yan et al. [1] proposed a new algorithm for automatic object segmentation in different color space. Gondra et al. [3] proposed a target segmentation algorithm based on machine learning. The gray image segmentation is highly efficient. The color image segmentation splits the image from different color spaces. Lowe [5][6] proposes a SIFT feature extraction algorithm with scale invariance. This algorithm is relatively stable in feature extraction and it can effectively deal with affine transformation and perspective transformation.

Each dolphin has its own characteristics, which can be used to distinguish different dolphins. In this paper, we improved the commonly used target segmentation algorithm and the identification algorithm and apply it to the field of dolphin image identification. We will present how to distinguish the identity of the dolphins through image recognition technology. We will present how to establish the identification model and the growth model of dolphins based on the surface characteristics of dolphins. We will also present an automatic management process of dolphins' image.

In Section 2, we will analyze dolphins target image segmentation. In Section 3, we will present image preprocessing and SIFT feature-matching algorithm. In Section 4, we will present our growth model. In Section 5, we will illustrate our experiments.

II. DOLPHINS TARGET IMAGE SEGMENTATION

In this paper, we need to segment the dolphins' targets from the background of sea image. However, there are a lot of waves on the ocean surface, which can lead to incorrect segmentation results. The color image segmentation divides the image from different color spaces, as in [3][4]. The image may be an image composed of multiple complex images, and the gray image segmentation may not divide the image, as in [1][2]. In this paper, we will propose two methods of using the color image segmentation:

1) Color image target segmentation;

2) Manual target segmentation.

The color image target segmentation technology uses an average clustering method. The dolphin image background is seen as a category and the dolphin target as another category. We used fuzzy C-means clustering methods to separate the dolphin image from the original color image. Then we obtained the dolphins' image target.

The implementation of the specific steps is as follows:

3) Determine the clustering center;

4) Adaptively determine the clustering center and classify the dolphins image according to the clustering strategy: sea background as class I and dolphins target as class II;

5) Separate class I from the dolphin in the image to obtain the dolphins of target class II.

We use the distribution of RGB color components as the scope of clustering in Figure 1. The integer value range of RGB three components is from 0 to 255. These points are contained within a quarter of the ball whose radius is 255; in Figure 1, the ordinate represents G component, the abscissa represents R component. Dolphin image pixel range is in the black line and blue line around the area. The scope of pixels of the water is in the red line and green line around the area.

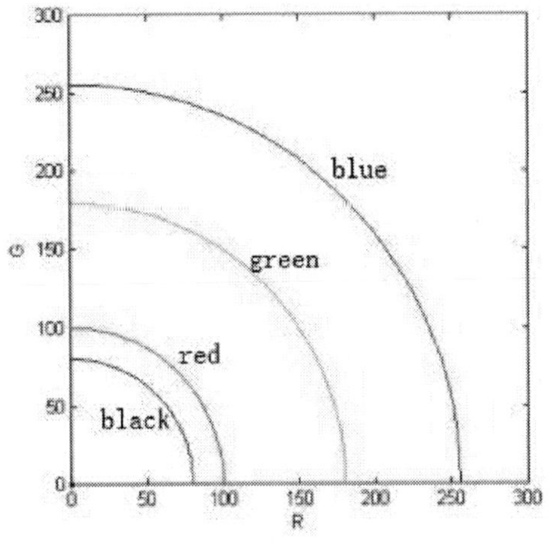

Figure 1. Scope of clustering

We calculated the maximum and the minimum Euclidean distances of each sampling matrix and the result is as follows:

$$L_{max}i = \max(L) \qquad L_{min}i = \min(L) \tag{1}$$

Calculate the maximum and minimum average distance:

$$\mu_{max} = \frac{\sum_{i=1}^{8} L_{max}i}{8} \qquad \mu_{min} = \frac{\sum_{i=1}^{8} L_{min}i}{8} \tag{2}$$

We also used the Euclidean distance to calculate the image color clustering center.

$$R_0 = \frac{\sum_{i=1}^{8} \mu_i}{8} \tag{3}$$

Where μ_i is each sampling matrix average Euclidean distance.

After calculating the Euclidean distance of all the pixels in the image, and comparing it with the clustering range, we regard the area within the scope as the sea background and the pixel is set to 0; the area that is beyond the scope is to keep the original pixel distribution. The results are shown in Figure 2.

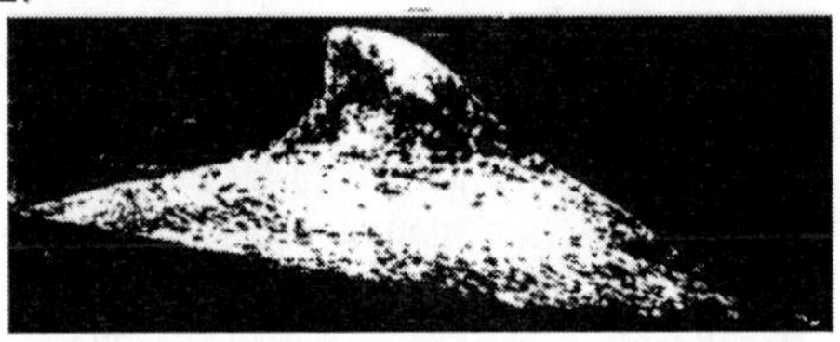

Figure 2. Image using color segmentation algorithm

Manual segmentation is done by manipulating the mouse on the image, as shown in Figure 3. The blue line in Figure 3a is the route of the mouse in manual segmentation. Figure 3b is the goal and Figure 3c is the result after the image segmentation. The steps of manual target segmentation are: Firstly, mark the needed segmented regions, and set the pixels of the image in the area to 1, the pixels of other areas of the image to 0. Then the template image of Figure 3b is obtained. Secondly, the result of the template image and original image multiplication is the target image after segmentation.

Figure 3. Manual target segmentation

Automatic target segmentation is more effective and has fewer human errors. But if the image quality is low and it needs higher segmentation precision, it is better to use manual target segmentation.

III. Image Preprocessing and SIFT Feature Matching Algorithm

In this section, we obtain the distribution of the spots on the surface of dolphins by image preprocessing, and then we can calculate these spots and establish the growth model of dolphins.

A. Image pre-processing phase

The spots on the surface of the dolphin are the feature points of the dolphin identification. The spots on the surface of the dolphin are dense and vary in size, which will increase computation of spots extraction, and produce errors easily. So we have taken three steps to preprocess: remove the edge; spot inflation; spot polymerization.

In this paper, we used Prewitt edge detection algorithm to process the dolphin image that has been segmented, and accurately detected the dolphins' surface spots edge. At the same time, manual segmentation region contour edge was detected. These contours can produce unnecessary interference to identify the effect, so it needs to be removed.

We used 5*5 square matrix corrosion structure elements. The target shape of the corrosion has not been changed, and the image edge was removed.

Now, the dolphins' surface spots are accurately marked out. However, the spots very in size and are unevenly distributed, which makes the statistics and identification prone to error. We carry out the result by expansion processing these spots, and make some small spots together, as a new feature point. The structural elements of expansion which we use is: $\begin{bmatrix} 0 & 0 & 1 & 0 & 0 \\ 0 & 1 & 1 & 1 & 0 \\ 1 & 1 & 1 & 1 & 1 \\ 0 & 1 & 1 & 1 & 0 \\ 0 & 0 & 1 & 0 & 0 \end{bmatrix}$. We carried out on the spots three times in the expansion operation.

We can see from the picture that small spots formed together big spots, and features are more obvious.

B. SIFT feature matching algorithm

SIFT (Scale Invariant Feature Transform) features keep the invariance to image scaling, rotation, scale brightness unchanged, which is a very stable local l feature, as in [7], thus has very extensive application value.

SIFT feature matching algorithm is used to identify the matching function that can be divided into three phases. The first stage is the feature point detection. Extract all of the images for matching feature points. The second stage is the feature descriptor. Add a detailed description for the local feature of the extracted feature points. The third stage is to generate the feature vector and feature vector match. Find out the mutual matching feature points by comparing the original image and the target image feature points, thus we could establish the corresponding relationship between objects.

We have found the key points and have given them position, scale and direction information. However, we need a special set of key vector to describe the key points of the image and the key points that include not only the key, but also include the pixels around the key points for its contributions. Descriptor will be used as the basis of target matching.

We took the 8 * 8 window centered on key points. The squares of window are divided into groups with size of 4 * 4, using statistical methods to obtain the gradient direction and gradient magnitude in each group. In the end, the gradient and direction of these different groups form a set of vectors. This group can be used to describe the key point and the descriptor. Being generated according to pixel of the key points in the field, the descriptors have strong inhibition to noise.

IV. Growth Model

Jefferson et al. [8] had proposed to divide the Chinese white dolphin into six age groups, but the boundary was not clear. It was also not clear how to represent the ages. The recognition criteria are shown in table I according to the different age paragraphs.

TABLE I. STANDARD OF DIFFERENT AGES

age grades	description
childhood and early youth	childhood skin color is dark gray, no spots, body length smaller, body length is about 1/3 to 1/2 of adult; early youth individuals is grey or light grey, and occasionally has dark spots, and is significantly greater than childhood, body length is about two-thirds of the adult.
youth and sub-adult	Complexion is pale, general is pale pink or white, with more spots, occasional dark spots.
adult	pure white or pink, less or no spots.

The change of Chinese white dolphins' spots and the change rule of age are shown in Figure 4. The horizontal axis is the dolphins' age, unit is the month. The vertical axis is the number of feature points of the dolphins' image detected.

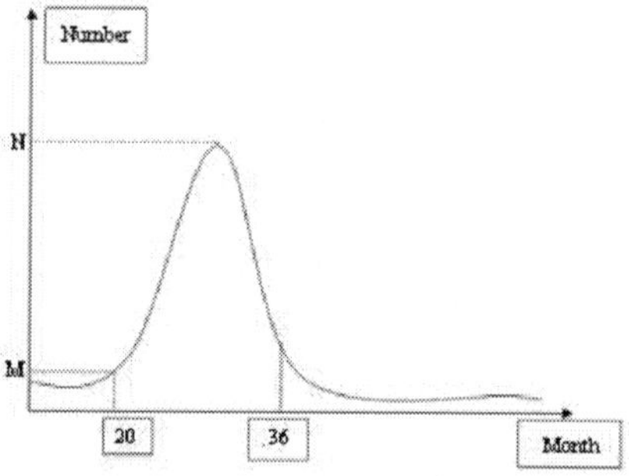

Figure 4. Dolphins spots variation

We can see that from born to 20 months old, the number of the dolphins' surface spots are sparse, and with the passage of time, the number of spots gradually increased. However, when dolphins are teenagers, there will be a substantial increase in growth of the number of spots. When the number of dolphins' surface spots reached a peak, the number of spots will decline rapidly. In the end, the spots of dolphins disappear or there are only a few spots, which is the sign of the maturation of the dolphin. So we can complete statistics of dolphins' age through statistics of the number of their surface spots. But among the spots on the surface of the dolphins, some are big and some are small. Therefore, we expand the small spots in the image. The spots shape characteristics are not changed when the small spots get together. The size and number of the spots on the surface of a dolphin are both the mark of a dolphin's age and identity.

For the experimental part, we used 190 dolphin images provided by the Pearl River estuary Dolphin Conservation base. 100 images are randomly selected from these images. Then the selected images are processed automatically by object segmentation, image preprocessing, and feature point extraction. Thus their feature points distributions are obtained, and then we obtain the images corresponding to their age. The results are shown in Figure 5 which is the age distribution of dolphins.

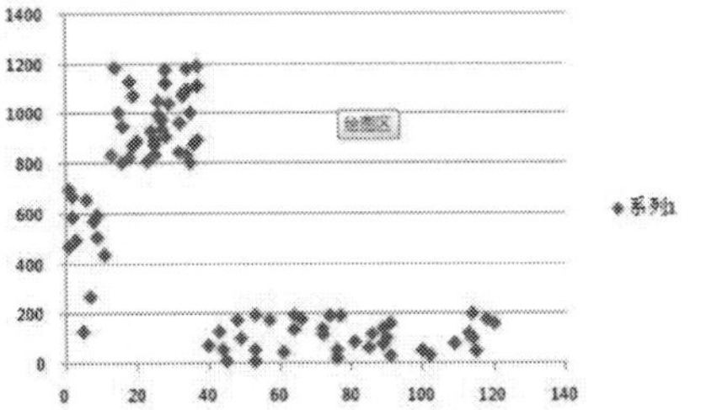

Figure 5. The age distribution of dolphins

There are three conclusions in Figure 5.

1) When the age of the dolphin is between 0 to 12 months old, the number of the key points detected on the dolphin's surface is between 200 and 760.

2) When the age of the dolphin is between 15 to 38 months old, the number of the key points detected on the dolphin's surface is between 800 and 1200.

3) When the dolphin's age is greater than 40 months, the number of the key points detected on the dolphin's surface is between 0 and 200.

V. EXPERIMENTS

In this paper, we used 190 images of the White Dolphin after artificial classification. Each image is attached with the age information. We use 90 images as the experimental object to verify the accuracy of the dolphins' growth model. 90 images were processed in order to extract the feature points, and to determine the age of dolphins according to the number of feature points. The results were compared with the results of the dolphin protection workers. Through the experiment, the correct rate using dolphins' growth model to estimate the age of the dolphins was 85%, the remaining 15% of the error rate is because there are some waves in the dolphins' image covering the key points. However, due to the high transparency of the waves, the human eye can see the spots on the surface of the dolphins through the spray, and identify the dolphin's age.

The matching strategy judges the dolphin's identity through key points. The dolphin's image matching experiment can be divided into three groups: normal image matching experiment, partial occlusion experiment, and rotating image experiment. Supposing the number of key points detected in the input image is M, the key points number of template is N, the number of the key to successfully match is K, and the matching rate is δ.

$$\delta = \frac{k}{N} * 100\% \tag{4}$$

A. Normal dolphin image matching

Figure 6. Normal dolphin image

The image needs to be identified as in Figure 6. The experiment selected 5 images as input image. The experimental results are shown in Table II.

TABLE II. EXPERIMENTAL RESULTS 1

Test image	M	N	K	δ	Recognition result
1	2759	3046	1797	0. 619	1
3	947	2054	76	0. 037	4
5	2896	3700	2176	0. 588	5
7	3315	4125	3110	0. 754	7
9	3689	2789	1706	0. 612	9

The matching rate of recognition is 80%.

B. partial occlusion experiment

Segmentation of the body surface features of a dolphin uses manual target segmentation. Then the segmented image is recognized. The segmented image is shown in Figure 7.

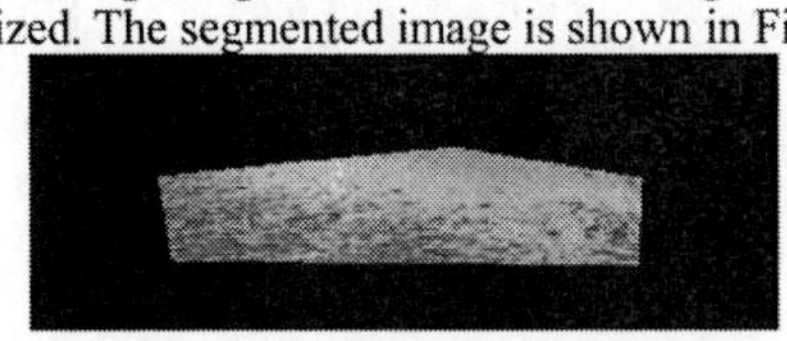

Figure 7. Partial occlusion of dolphin image

Partial target segmentation of pictures No. 1, 3, 5, 7, 9 images, experimental results are in Table III.

TABLE III. EXPERIMENTAL RESULTS 2

Test image	M	N	K	δ	Recognition result
1	446	3046	136	0. 305	4
3	987	2054	575	0. 583	3
5	1783	3700	1101	0. 621	5
7	2596	4125	477	0. 184	9
9	1865	2789	1108	0. 594	9

The experimental results show that the matching rate is 60%.

C. Rotation matching experiment

Rotate No. 1, 3, 5, 7, 9 and match recognition, as shown in Figure 8.

Figure 8. Rotating image

Experimental results are illustrated in Table IV.

TABLE IV. EXPERIMENTAL RESULTS 4

Test image	M	N	K	δ	Recognition result
1	2786	3046	1739	0. 571	1
3	1486	2054	1051	0. 512	3
5	3412	3700	1161	0. 314	7
7	3752	4125	2397	0. 581	7
9	2163	2789	1484	0. 533	9

The matching rate of the experimental result was 80%.

After more than three sets of experiments, it can be shown when the rotation, occlusion and other factors influence the image; the recognition rate is still higher than 60%. SIFT feature extraction algorithm is very effective in the use of dolphin identification.

VI. CONCLUSION

In this paper, we have studied the dolphin image segmentation, the image preprocessing, and key point detection. Then, we summed up the relationship between the key quantity and dolphin age, and the dolphin growth model. Through the experiment, we used a dolphin growth model to estimate the age of the dolphins and the correct rate was 85%. Finally, the key points can be used to accurately describe the characteristics of the image. The accuracy of the dolphin matching is measured, and the accuracy rate is above 60%. In this paper, the growth model of dolphins established by key points can estimate the age of dolphins by the number of key points. But when the part of the key points of dolphins' surface are covered, the result is not accurate. In the future, we will study how to use probability estimation to estimate the dolphin's age when the key points of the dolphin are covered.

ACKNOWLEDGMENT

This research is supported by (1) 2017-2020 The National Natural Science Fund (Project No. 51679058). (2) 2013-2016 China Higher Specialized Research Fund (PhD supervisor category) (20132304110018).

REFERENCES

[1] L. Jun, M. Yan, and C. Kun, "Adaptive color image segmentation based on multi color spatial component, " computer engineering and application 50(5). pp. 185-189, 2014.

[2] H. Trung and Manh, "Small object segmentation based on visual saliency in natural images, " 2013Journal of Information Processing Systems, v 9, n 4. pp. 592-601, 2013.

[3] I. Gondra, T. Xu, D. Chiu, and M. Cormier, "Object segmentation through multiple instance learning, " Lecture Notes in Computer Science, v 8509 LNCS. pp. 568-577, 2014.

[4] B. Sirmacek and C. Unsalan, "Urban-Area and Building Detection Using SIFT Key points and Graph Theory, " IEEE Transactions on Geosciences and Remote sen-sing 47(4). pp. 562, 2009.

[5] L. Canlin and M. Lizhuang, "A new framework for feature descriptor based on SIFT, " Pattern Recognition Letters 30. pp. 544-547, 2009.

[6] J. Mohammad, M. Sami, and S. Gaurav, "Multi-image stitching and scene reconstruction for evaluating defect evolution in structures, " Structural Health Monitoring 10(6). pp. 643-646, 2011.

[7] Z. Morteza and M. S. Seyed, "License plate recognition system based on SI-FT features, " Procedia Computer Science 3. pp. 998-999, 2011.

[8] T. Jefferson and S. Leatherwood, Distribution and abundance of Indo-Pacific humpbacked dolphins (Sousa chinensis) in Hong Kong waters. Asian Marine Biology 14. pp. 93-100, 1997.

Visual Public Protection Disaster Relief and Critical Infrastructure

(Visual PCI)

Aurel Machalek, Dominic Dunlop, Carlo Simon, Ralf Hoben
University of Luxembourg
Interdisciplinary Centre for Security, Reliability and Trust
Luxembourg, Luxembourg
email: firstname.lastname@uni.lu

***Abstract*— A 2013 Decision of the European Parliament and of the Council requires relevant national and appropriate sub-national level authorities to establish risk assessments covering the full spectrum of consequences. These may be expressed in terms of human, environmental, economic, and political/social impacts. Modern society is increasingly dependent on critical infrastructure and on the services that it provides. The loss of one of these services may hit the public immediately in manners which are not always predictable. Furthermore, the amount of time that a given service is unavailable will affect other services through numerous direct and indirect dependencies, which are seldom considered. Natural or man-made disasters, and combinations of both, will have effects that are difficult or impossible to foresee without the appropriate tools. Due to the rapid progress in electronic communications and information technology, one would expect today's crisis managers to have access to situational awareness and to the tools needed to inform their decisions. While much has been achieved for single-service operational headquarters like those of police, firefighting and ambulance services, there are no solutions that address the interactions and interdependencies of all critical functions and all critical infrastructure in a Public Protection and Disaster Response context. If a crisis develops when some aspect of critical infrastructure is partly or completely unavailable, crisis managers must make decisions using a very different framework compared to that used to handle limited incidents in normal times. Considering the difficulties resulting from the dependencies and interdependencies of critical infrastructure in normal times, making good decisions is becoming more and more difficult for crisis managers during a crisis. These challenges, combined with the enormous and possibly tragic consequences of suboptimal crisis management, provide good reasons to explore the subject.**

Keywords-component; Visualisation; Augmented Reality; Augmented desktop; Data visualisation; 2D/3D Visualisation

I. INTRODUCTION

The main objective and ambition of the Visual Protection of Critical Infrastructure (Visual PCI) project is to create a coherent system for visualisation of all crisis management activities and assets able to handle full real-life complexity. There are many existing visualisation systems for specific aspects of crisis management, but all are strictly focused on their own narrow slice of the crisis management domain. Our goal is extremely ambitious: there is no known system capable of visualising all aspects of a crisis management situation simultaneously.

Visual PCI's ambition is to provide a novel and integrated tool for risk assessment, planning activities and crisis management at international, national, and appropriate sub-national levels.

The value of a system as a whole is generally much greater than the sum of the values of its parts considered in isolation: it is much better to have a car than just to have four wheels. The same is true for IT systems and simulation systems. A system capable of coherently simulating or visualising several aspects of a phenomena can also take into account interdependencies and feedback between those aspects, so raising the quality of simulation or visualisation to an entirely new level.

Consequently, the main value of Visual PCI is to create a coherent visualisation system capable of handling multiple aspects of crisis management at the same time, in accordance with selection criteria applied by the end user. Such a wider view will allow the end user to perceive interdependencies between various crisis-related phenomena and activities that could otherwise pass unnoticed. Thus the project will allow an appreciation of a crisis situation having a completeness far beyond the abilities of any existing system. The project's primary contribution is to allow interaction with – and visualisation of – the multiple layers that are relevant under disaster emergency conditions. The project will also build on the work done in the coMap project[1], which explored the specific roles which people should have when making decisions using table-top visualisation systems, and how such policies can be enforced.

If accepted by relevant end users, at national or even European level, Visual PCI has the potential to influence standardisation activities, as implied by [2], [3], and [4].

Because Visual PCI will rely on standards already used at a European level, data input from statistics and geospatial data will be facilitated, and previously-developed models may be used with no or little modification by all implementations. Thus, the use of Visual PCI in Member States is facilitated, while a federation of implementations may serve at European level.

Visual PCI will be designed to be used in different configurations comprising:

- A stand-alone solution,
- Multiple identical implementations in a distributed architecture to maximise Information Assurance by means of redundancy,
- Inside a federation to allow exchange between neighbouring implementations,

- In a hierarchical structure able to respond to organisational concepts and to provide scalability, and
- Any combination of these.

II. RELATED WORK

The Visual PCI project is aware of some recent projects in related areas of national risk assessment, public protection and disaster response as well as critical infrastructure. The following projects have been analysed for their relevance; Visual PCI differs from all of these in the novelty of its integrated tool for risk assessment, activity planning, and crisis management at international, national and appropriate sub-national level, accommodating human, environmental, economic and political/social impacts.

CRISADMIN: Critical Infrastructure Simulation of Advanced Models on Interconnected Networks resilience [5], was concerned with the evaluation of the impact of large catastrophic events, such as terrorist attacks on critical infrastructure, by deploying/developing a decision support system.

THREVI2: Threat-Vulnerability Path Identification for Critical Infrastructures [6] focussed on: identification of potential hazards and threats to CI systems; assessing the vulnerability of CI systems or components against these hazards; and defining accurate scenarios.

FACIES: Online Identification of Failure and Attack on Interdependent Critical Infrastructures [7] defined cooperation strategies for automatic detection of failures and attacks on CI, by promptly identifying a failure and/or attack on several interdependent types of critical infrastructure.

CISIM set out to improve an existing framework for simulating the resilience of critical information and communication technologies of CT) infrastructure against threats, such as power failures, floods and terrorist attacks.

DISASTER 2.0: This project [8] investigated ways of strengthening public resilience to disasters by identifying: technologies, such as social media and semantic webs, that government organisations use to communicate with the public; innovative ways in which these technologies have been used; and how the public use these technologies during disasters.

CRISMA: Modelling crisis management for improved action and preparedness [9], this project focused on large scale crisis scenarios with often irreversible immediate and extended human, societal, structural and economic consequences and impacts. The project developed a simulation-based decision support system for modelling crisis management, aiding improved action and preparedness.

DRIVER: The Driving Innovation in Crisis Management for European Resilience) project [10] is developing an environment that will allow research and innovation to flourish in crisis management. The experiments that it enables may inform the building of scenarios for Visual PCI.

Finally, the use of a multi-touch table in disaster management is explored in [11]; this is just one aspect of the remit of Visual PCI.

Blue: Highways with interchanges
Red: Power supply network with transformers
Orange: Power distribution areas

Figure 1. Visual PCI 3D Model representing Luxembourg

III. VISUALISATION

The rapid development approach to a risk assessment support tool through visualisation with the early involvement of end users is the key to the success of Visual PCI. Visualisation of model building, data input, situational awareness and simulation is essential for user ergonomics. While the basic components for visualisation must be developed by IT professionals, it is also necessary that trained end users can add and modify elements in order to refine the models. Visualisation will provide confidence to end users about their ability to use Visual PCI and to improve the solution over time by fine-tuning the models. Visualisation will produce confidence in making risk assessments by allowing the navigation of risk chains through mouse clicks in order to check the origins of given risks and their impacts. Visualisation will also support situational awareness by producing maps with overlays providing relevant information about incidents, Public Protection and Disaster Relief (PPDR) resources and critical infrastructure services. Finally, Visual presentation of alternative courses of action will support crisis managers' decision process.

For example, the visualisation of Fig. 1 illustrates the dependency of the road network on electrical power. During blackouts, the lack of security services in tunnels, of illumination, and of control by traffic lights reduces the capacity of the road network.

The visualisations will also show time-driven effects like the build-up of traffic jams or changes in strategic fuel stocks. Slow and fast motion can be used as required by end users.

Visual PCI requires the following components:

- A robust visualisation component to facilitate the input and interpretation of information, the adaptation of models and the creation of scenarios to provide planning support for working groups and situational awareness and decision support for crisis managers. Fig. 2 shows a possible visualisation of an urban area.

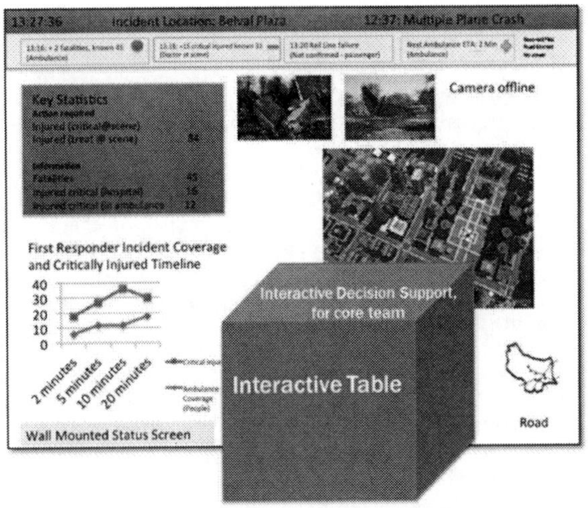

Figure 2. Visual PCI scenario

- A database holding statics and discrete information regarding population, environment, economic and political/social aspects, as well critical infrastructure and PPDR elements. The data required will be driven by the area of responsibility of the implementing end user.
- A computation environment, allowing the models to compute risk assessments and to run simulations regarding the impact of threats and hazards.
- A lightweight and flexible interface infrastructure for heterogeneous data sources allowing the updating of relevant data from different stakeholders, including real-time data from sensors.
- A document-generation capacity to produce periodical and updated risk assessments as required by end users.

IV. VISUALISATION: POSSIBLE SCENARIO

The following section explains how a planning group would use the interface during an incident.

As seen in the background of the figure 2, the interface consists of a large display providing selected information about a plane crash for the entire planning group, while an interactive table is used by a reduced number of people from the core team to make the actual decisions. The types of screen provided by Visual PCI will be in line with identified user requirements.

The large, wall-mounted display provides key statistics, still and live pictures showing the incident, the evolution over time of the number of victims confirmed and remaining at the site, and the first responder coverage capacity at the site. In the lower right, the functional layer of the highway system shows possible access routes and the expected delays ambulances will encounter. Zooming into the incident area provides details of the chosen location.

The concept of Visual PCI will allow planning groups to input a minimum of data to set the scene for a scenario. Once the site and the date/time have been chosen, Visual PCI is able to extract from its database the information required to display the vicinity of the scenario, to estimate the traffic situation and to provide the probable number of people around the site. (This is not an exhaustive list of possible data types.) The information will be presented immediately in a way which is designed to avoid information overload and to reduce the time needed to reach decisions.

The team will then input the data relating to the incident. In the case of a plane crash, it is necessary to provide the number and categories of victims. The presumed injuries of the survivors will dictate the urgent work load of the rescuers. It will also be possible to predict the time necessary to register the victims and thus provide this information with a delay (as in real world accidents). Weather conditions may be chosen as a function of the season.

Visual PCI will show the PPDR resources available to intervene on the site, such as police patrols, ambulance crews and firefighters active or on standby in the region. The data available on traffic density and the weather conditions will dictate the travelling times to the scene. The use of blue lights by the emergency services will be considered by the simulation.

In risk assessment mode, Visual PCI will use a model response to simulate the evacuation of wounded people to hospitals. This simulation may then be repeated by Visual PCI for varying crash sites, number of wounded people and date/timing considerations.

The same scenario may be used for training crisis managers. In this setting, the model will wait for trainee input before dispatching PPDR resources. Fig. 3 provides a possible screenshot of the interactive table during training. Visual PCI may be configured to provide to the trainee key with information about predicted outcomes of possible decisions. Those may include traffic information or reduced emergency service efficiency for non-optimal options. This function will speed up training and enhance the confidence of the trainee through the provision of visual feedback.

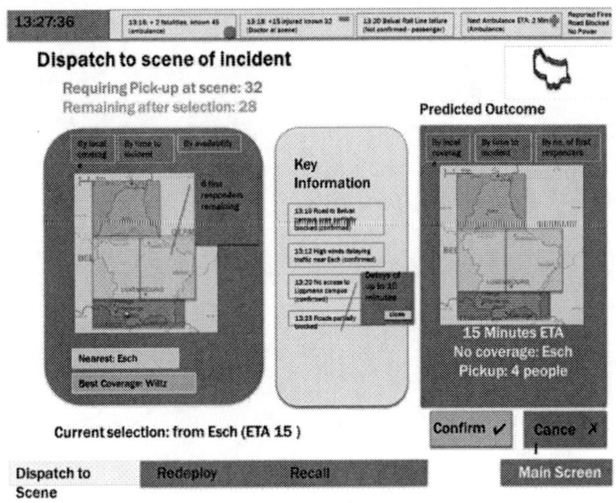

Figure 3. Visual PCI scenario interactive table display

In planning mode, selected scenarios developed by particular planning groups may be used by planning boards having differing vocations and expertise. This multi-disciplinary approach will enhance overall effectiveness.

The Visual PCI system will make use of a variety of technologies. For example, we expect to use Kivy[1] (an open source Python library) to allow for interaction on the multi-touch surface. Kivy is also cross-platform, ensuring that the outputs of the project are not tied to a particular vendor.

Additionally, an appropriate 3D modelling/game environment, such as Unity 3D[2] or perhaps open source alternatives such as Crystal Space[3] will be considered. In order to allow for iterative and rapid development, high level programming languages such as Python or Ruby will be used.

V. Conclusion

Visual PCI will simplify and optimise risk management, planning and crisis management and therefore speed up recovery and costs and the number of victims. But Visual PCI will bring even more:

Visual PCI will know the local critical infrastructure and its dependencies and interdependencies. It has the capabilites being adaptable to local circumstances and of following the evolution of the infrastructure.

While Visual PCI is for crisis managers, the tool may also be used to detect infrastructure weaknesses and to predict future bottlenecks if fast-growing infrastructure outpaces the evolution of supporting structures. Therefore, Visual PCI has the potential to assist not only in risk assessments and PPDR planning, but also in national or regional development activities.

Visual PCI has the potential to influence the development of European Resilience Management Guidelines and demonstration through its pilot implementation.

References

[1] S. Tarik and S. A. P. Ag, "Support for Collaborative Situation Analysis and Planning in Crisis Management Teams using Interactive Tabletops," Proc. 2013 ACM international conference on Interactive tabletops and surfaces, pp. 273–282, ISBN: 978-1-4503-2271-3.

[2] "Decision No 1313/2013/EU of the European Parliament and of the Council of 17 December 2013 on a Union Civil Protection Mechanism," Official Journal of the European Union, L 347, 20.12.2013, pp. 924–947, ISSN: 1977-0677.

[3] International Electrotechnical Commission (IEC), International Organization for Standardization (ISO), "Risk Management — Risk Assessment Techniques," (IEC/ISO 31010:2009), ISO, Geneva, Switzerland.

[4] "SEC (2010) 1626 Final Commission Staff Working Paper, Risk Assessment and Mapping Guidelines for Disaster Management," European Commission, 2010.

[5] S. Armenia et al., "CRitical Infrastructure Simulation of ADvanced Models on Interconnected Networks resilience — Final Report," FORMIT Foundation, Rome, Italy, 2014.

[6] F. Naghali, "Creating an ontology for critical infrastructures topology and assets taxonomy," PhD thesis, Politecnico Milano, Italy, 2013.

[7] E. E. Miciolino, R. Setola, F. Pascucci, J. Lopez, M. M. Polycarpou, "FACIES: a Testbed for Distributed Fault and Attack Identification in Interdependent Critical Infrastructures," 2nd International SCADA LAB Workshop, Seville, Spain, 2014.

[8] R. Beneito-Montagut, D. Shaw, C. Brewster, "Disaster 2.0: Emergency Management Agencies use and adoption of Web 2.0," Aston University, UK, 2013.

[9] A. Garcia-Aristizabal et al., "Dynamic scenario concept models", 2013. [Online]. Available from: http://www.crismaproject.eu.

[10] "DRIVER: Innovation in crisis mamanagement," Crisis Response Journal, vol. 11, no. 3, p. 86, March 2013.

[11] K. Nebe, F. Klompmaker, H. Jung, and H. Fischer, "Exploiting new interaction techniques for disaster control management using multitouch-, tangible- and pen-based-interaction," Proc. 14th international conference on Human-computer interaction: interaction techniques and environments, Part II, pp. 100–109, 2011, ISBN: 978-3-642-21604-6

[1] https://kivy.org

[2] https://unity3d.com

[3] http://crystalspace3d.org

Full Incremental Learning for Along Classification of Textual Images

Vincent Poulain d'Andecy
L3i, University of La Rochelle
and ITESOFT Group – Yooz
La Rochelle, France
email:vincent.poulaindandecy@yooz.fr

Aurélie Joseph and Saddok Kebairi
Research and Technologies Department
ITESOFT Group – Yooz
Aimargues, France
email:{aurelie.joseph, saddok.kebairi}@yooz.fr

Abstract— **Incremental classification is still a challenge with an important industrial impact by allowing a class training process simplification. Recently, works on Incremental Growing Neural Gas (IGNG) have demonstrated the ability of this technology to cope with this challenge for Optical Character Recognition(OCR)-based image classification. Previous proposals focused on the classifier itself but did not deal with descriptors which were not in the scope of these studies taking an a priori fixed descriptors set. This assumption is not applicable in real-life when the environment is progressive and the incremental system does not know a priori the image content to learn. In this paper we proposed an enhancement of an incremental system based on an IGNG extension (A2ING) with a combination of graphical, re-using the Blurred Shape Model (BSM), and a novel strategy based on incremental textual descriptors. Performance achievement shows a better precision with an acceptable recall than predefined descriptors. The benefit is to not require a prior descriptors selection.**

Keywords-incremental classification; text-based vector; shape-based vector; BSM; A2ING; Document Image Processing.

I. INTRODUCTION

Even if more and more documents are managed by electronic exchanges, the paper document is still used and need an image capture for automatic processing. Moreover, the increasing use of mobile devices generates nowadays a large volume of images which can be digitized papers (receipts, etc.) or natural scene image with text (a board, an advertisement, etc.) all so-called documents. It is an industrial challenge to classify all these images for indexing, archiving or business processing. In this paper, we are interested in supervised image classification containing textual information.

Currently, we use an OCR-based system with a supervised classifier. Each class is known and for the training, we have representative images preprocessed by the OCR. A word-class pair weight is calculated to extract specific words featuring the document classes. Thus, learning algorithms calculate the proximity between images and predict which class the document belongs to. We can use different standard algorithms: Support Vector Machine (SVM), Naïves Bayes, K-Nearest Neighbour (k-NN).

To set-up these systems, we need an a priori groundtruth with labelled document by class. These methods are usually efficient but we face to limitations and new needs:

- adding easily a new class in the system,
- discovering new data along the process,
- reducing the number of sample,
- processing big data.

Incremental classification approaches [9] can theoretically manage these issues. Similarly to supervised approaches, incremental classification systems require a feature vector to model the problem. For instance, an image can be represented by its pixels. For a text-based document, the vector could be a bag-of-words. As we will see for this last case, an issue lies in the selection of these words. The number of descriptors is problematic as well. How many have to be selected to represent our vector, knowing that the vector length cannot be growing?

Proposals on incremental classification are numerous [6][10][14]. We chose to use the Active Incremental Growing Neural Gas (A2ING) algorithm which is one of most recent proposals. Our contribution is not yet on the A2ING itself but we propose a novel method based on the A2ING to classify incrementally textual document without a priori knowledge using both a shape-based vector and a dynamic text-based vector discovering significant words throughout the process.

In section II, we introduce the A2ING and some related systems. Hence, we describe our system enhancement in section III and comment our results in section IV. Perspectives are given as conclusion in section V.

II. RELATED WORKS

Incremental classification is not a new method in machine learning. Basically, incremental classification learns along the process to cover the samples representation space according to given descriptors. Its benefits are plural. As it learns along the process, it does not need all necessary classes at the beginning and thus, can discover new data. When a class has enough elements to classify documents, it stops asking the class label to the user [9]. So, we can reduce the number of sample for each class.

Polikar et al.[14] gives an overview of several algorithms for incremental classification. Some of them are an evolution of classical algorithms (incremental SVM [12], Incremental K-means [15]). Other approaches are based on Incremental Growing Neural Gas (IGNG) and variations like the one proposed by Hamza & al.[6] for clustering (unsupervised classification). Among IGNG family, Bouguelia & al.[9][10] have proposed an incremental semi-supervised classifier (A2ING). This system is introduced below (Figure 1).

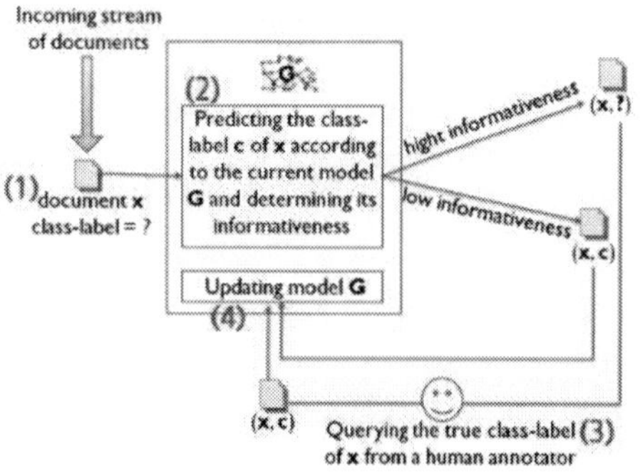

Figure 1. Rafik Bouguelia's A2ING general scheme[10].

(1) Each object X is represented as a vector. When an unknown object X is classified (2), according to an informativeness criteria, the object is rejected (3) for user annotation or predicted to a class C. During the annotation (3) the user can give an existing class reinforcing (4) the system or create dynamically a new class to expend the system scope (4).

Theoretically, the system is never ending. It adapts itself due to the ability of introducing a new class on real-time.

Drawbacks, all these different algorithms rely on a set of fixed descriptors to feature all classes, usually, a vector X representing the object to classify. The performance comes from both the classifier and the feature vector to figure out discriminations. In all the quoted references, different feature vectors are used showing the flexibility of the classifier to various problems. Bouguelia [9] experimented normalized snippet pixels to feature characters, temporal and spatial features for on-line characters, bag-of-words for textual documents, etc. In any case, the vector is defined a priori, fixed size and hence, it closes obviously the ability to feature a new problem. For instance, when using a bag-of-words which does not include English words, you cannot classify a document written in English.

Literature offers many descriptor proposals oriented for the classification purpose: for detecting human being in a scene, we can use gradients, colours information [11]; for handwriting/machine print classification, we can measure linearity and profile regularity on pseudo words [16]; for logo classification or document classification, we can use a Blurred Shape Model [3] or pixel density quantification on patches [4]; for structure document classification, layout feature or structural features can be used [2]; LLAH approaches for retrieving textual documents [7]; and weighted bag-of-words for text classification [5]. Bag-of-words are usually large vectors of words where each word defines a dimension.

To summarize all these experiences, graphical or pixel based descriptors are fine for structured information (forms, logo, tables, etc.) but less efficient in case of variable document structures (news, emails, etc.). Text-based descriptors are more robust to the document structure variation, allowing natural language text classification. These descriptors are words or group of words supposed to be discriminant for the classification. To select this lexicon, a previous statistical analysis of the domain is required. Basically, Term Frequency (TF) and Inverse Document Frequency (IDF) methods [5] can be applied.

According to us, the definition of the feature vector for the incremental classification of textual images is a bottleneck. Moreover, we cannot plan neither the domain nor the structure of any new image class appearing along our process.

Hamza and al.[6] and Bouguelia and al.[10] successfully experimented textual features (bag-of-words) for textual documents incremental classification. However, they never discussed the lexicon selection because this topic was not in the center of their works. They suppose a preprocessing stage to define the vector before to start the incremental learning. Here, a prior TF analysis on text samples was performed to select words for the vector. This preprocessed word learning stage is contradictory with our incremental classification objectives. An additional difficulty is that the feature vector proposed for the A2ING shall be fixed-size. This is due to the used vector distance function (cosine or euclidian). Notice the similar issue for many standard classifiers (SVM, Perceptron…). But obviously, the bag-of-words dimension depends on the variability and complexity of the corpus vocabulary. It differs from a domain to another. [5] demonstrates on different corpus (Popol and Reuters) the impact of the vector dimension on classification results. A generic model cannot be a fixed-size vector.

Deep Learning approaches [17][18] offer today a strategy to avoid the explicit feature selection. For instance, quoted reference authors apply deep learning for text understanding from character-level inputs. They use temporal convolutional networks to let the system discovers relevant features. Even if this approach is interesting, it is not yet compatible for incremental learning based on few samples discovered along the process.

As described above, image analysis approaches provide generic structural and holistic descriptors but they are inefficient and difficult to tune [4] for poorly structured documents. Unfortunately, they often appear in our image workflow (receipts, invoices, bank notice, payslips, etc.)

To cope with this challenge, we design an innovative and real full incremental system for textual document images.

III. PROPOSAL

We propose to combine a standard shape-based descriptor and an original adaptive and generic textual descriptor with the A2ING.

A. *Shape-based classification*

Many shape-based descriptors are compliant to document incremental classifiers because they can be fully computed during the process, they are fixed-size, and they are independent of the document semantic or the document content (genericity). For all these reason, we propose to use a shape-based vector. One of them is the Blurred Shape Model (BSM)[3]. The BSM splits the picture in 8x8 squares and each square is calculating from a blur pixel representation. We have chosen this method due the simplicity and the demonstrated efficiency on various document image classification problems: structured document classification, and logo classification [8].

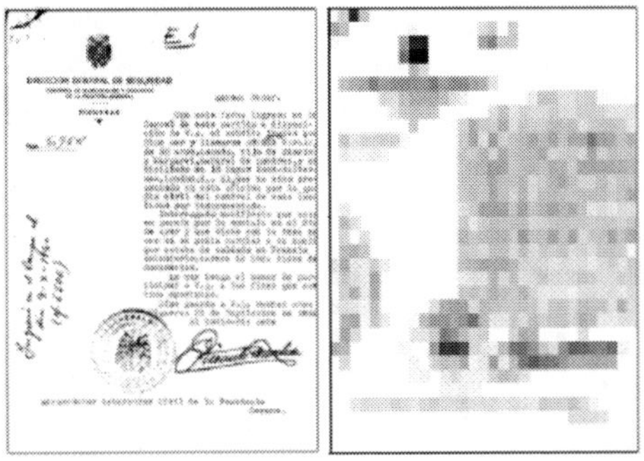

Figure 2. Example of blurred image by the BSM

But, this method is not efficient on semi-structured textual document because in this case the information is more carried by the text and words than the structure itself.

B. Text-based classification

Hence, a text-based vector for textual classification is an alternative method when the classification depends on accurate semantic textual information. Secondly, we can have documents (text in a natural scene) without recurrent structural information.

In the initial A2ING, the text based vector is pre computed. Our proposal is to enhance the system by dynamically discovering and expending the dimension of the text-based vector along the system life.

At the beginning, the feature vector X of the A2ING is empty (no dimension). Then, the vector X_i with i dimension is enlarged by n dimensions ($X_{i+n} = X_i \cup w_n$) when a set w_n of n "relevant" words are discovered to model a new class. This definition is compatible with an Euclidian distance because w_n new features are valued to 0 for any existing classes (already modelled by the X_i vector). At this stage, any new classes will be modelled by the X_{i+n} vector.

The issue is both to discover the w_n features and to decide when the text-based vector dimension shall be enlarged.

The discovery of relevant words for text classification is not a new topic. There are several statistical metrics in the state-of-the-art to figure out the relevance of words in a corpus. The most well-known method [5] is based on the Term Frequency / Inverse Document Frequency (TF/IDF). Basically, selected words are those frequent for one class and not frequent in all the others. It means selected words are discriminative. A more semantic method named Latent Semantic Analysis is used to make correlations between words in a document. It produces topic features instead of word features. Finally, these methods calculate a weight of a word or a concept to rank them. The selection is given by the top weights according to the ranking.

These statistic approaches need a representative training set to model several variables: language, domain, classes, etc. In our case, all these issues cannot be pre-defined because we do not know anything about captured images.

Bouillot [5] demonstrates that there is no best solution for all the cases but the only metric which is both dependent of an image class and independent of others is the Term Frequency. Far to be the best metric, TF is interesting because it can be computed incrementally each times a new sample appears without constraint from other classes and future unknown classes.

In this study, we propose the Term Frequency as a first approach for the w_n evaluation.

Most m frequent terms $W_m(k)$ for a class k give some key recurrent features for an image sample of the class. Statistically, we except $W_m(k)$ to be included (at least partially) within the terms of the image related to k. Let suppose we have j dimensions for the feature vector X_j, the vector T_j is the terms of an image limited to the identified X_j features and $X_j(k)$ is the A2ING instanced model vector for a class k:

the distance $D(k)=T_j. X_j(k)$ is minimized for the class k when $W_m(k)$ is included in X_j because $W_m(k)$ should be included in T_j as explained above. Then, the A2ING can predict this class.

If $W_m(k)$ is not included in X_j, the distance D(k) is maximized and the informativeness criteria of the A2ING will reject the prediction. In this case $X_{j+m} = X_j \cup W_m(k)$ will minimize D for the class k and in the same time may maximize D for any other class. The prediction is enhanced. The feature vector is dynamically enlarged.

The issue is to select the n terms w_n among $W_m(k)$ to add to the vector X. In this first study we propose to limit w_n to the n words with the best TF value for the class k and which are not yet in X when an image prediction is rejected. Actually, we set n to 1 to get the most frequent term not yet in X representing k. But it may happen that few terms occur always together due to an equal TF. With this strategy, we introduce a minimum number of "best" terms. If added terms are sufficient and discriminative to predict the class, then the incremental classification is optimal, otherwise the system will wait for further samples. The system will manage itself up to a sufficient number of terms to predict a class.

What happens if the system can never learn an image class and the X vector increase as infinite? This could be dramatic, moreover if image class samples occur frequently. To be honest, we have not yet deal with this question which is a perspective. For the moment we threshold the system to a maximum number of M considering that if the system cannot learn an image class with M Terms means the class is unpredictable.

Another difficult question is to decide when $W_m(k)$ is relevant. If only few images were captured for a class k, W(k) is not representative. Waiting for more samples to take a decision will delay the incremental learning, by keeping X out of W(k) inputs. This question is still to be explored. We have not yet found out a solution and we work around with a parameter giving a minimum number of samples to threshold the TF. This parameter can be set by experiments.

C. Multi-classifier-based classification

We can describe our system by the figure 3 below.

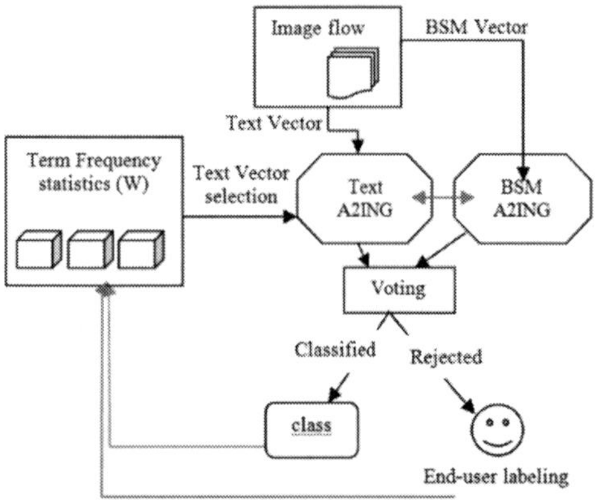

Figure 3. Schema of classification process

The BSM vector is computed directly on the image. The text classifier needs an OCR processing to compute the Text Vector X. The combination of both is a cooperative-concurrent classifiers.

1) Concurrent classifiers

Each classifier is an A2ING based classifier allowing parallel incremental learning. Each one has its own feature vectors: BSM Vector and Text Vector.

2) Cooperative classifiers

Both A2ING deliver a class prediction. Each answer (red link in figure 3) can be used as a feedback for the other to learn without waiting for the end-user feedback. End-user feedback or classification success enables the TF computation for the Text Vector selection (if needed).

IV. Result Comparison

We have experimented our proposal on the ITESOFT corpus that Bouguelia used for its measures. We describe this corpus below. Reusing this corpus, we can compare our proposal to the "a priori" defined textual vector as in [9][10].

A. Dataset

The ITESOFT corpus is available on demand according a NDA. Images are machine-printed document like invoices, mails, forms, etc. We have both TIF images and OCR readings. Thus, we can easily use shape and text vectors.

The corpus includes two datasets so-called MMA and LIRMM. MMA contains 2591 images divided on 25 classes. LIRMM contains 1951 images and 24 classes. To compare with Bouguelia, the dataset is splitted in two parts:

- Learning phase: to initialize a classifier and do not measure from scratch because the lack of samples biaised the measure. We take 2/3 of the dataset.
- Test phase: measure on remaining documents (1/3 of the corpus) while the classifier continues to learn.

B. Results on different approaches

We evaluate each single A2ING and the combination (table 1). We compare to initial Bouguelia works (table 2). For the quantification of the classification performance, we used the standard Recall and Precision measures like in [9].

TABLE I. Classification results with different approaches

	LIRMM dataset		MMA dataset	
	Recall (%)	*Precision (%)*	*Recall (%)*	*Precision (%)*
BSM	57	98	31	96
Text	78	96	62	96
Multi	82	98	66	93

BSM has the worst performance because the corpus contains mainly semi-structured documents. This vector is efficient only on very structured images. Hence the performance of the Multi-classifier really comes from the Text-classifier. However, BSM is useful for a part of the dataset: few classes with structured images and very few instances of image. In this case, the TF does not reach our threshold to be learnt by the Text-classifier.
Result difference between LIRMM and MMA is explained by different corpus complexity (more variability [9]).

C. Comparison with previous work.

Results "[9]" for the comparison between the non-generic vector A2ING and our proposal come from Bouguelia report [9].

TABLE II. Results with our proposal and Bouguelia approach

	LIRMM dataset		MMA dataset	
	Recall (%)	*Precision (%)*	*Recall (%)*	*Precision (%)*
Proposal	82	98	66	93
[9]	95,2	95,6	75	78,4

Unquestionably, recall is much better with Bouguelia approach while the precision is better with our system. However, performances are quite acceptable when you consider that the system started from scratch. It demonstrates both that descriptors can be learnt incrementally and that an A2ING can cope with a growing feature vector.

Our analysis shows two important reasons of the reduced performance:

- First comes for the selection of the vector X. Only based on the TF metric, iteratively updated by image along the processing of each dataset, we cannot converge to the same dictionary than a pre-computed TF/IDF. The table III demonstrates the difference. In our proposal we retrieve more than 91% of the TF/IDF dictionary from [9]. This is very good but we introduce a lot of unexpected additional words. They are for instance named entities (first name, last name, city names, etc.) or unrelevant words (natural langage syntactic operator like "like" "you", "of", "the"...) occurring in many images. For MMA the text variability is larger hence many best frequent words are not so frequents even if they are still the best frequent. The impact is to increase the D distance and in consequence the rejection. Positively it impacts the precision but it is a side effect.

TABLE III. FEATURE VECTOR SIZE COMPARISON

	LIRMM dataset	MMA dataset
Features vector in [9]	277	292
Our features vector	341	1700
Rate of features in [9] included in our	91%	93%

- A second reason is the learning delay of our approach. First learnt classes are re-learnt during the process because the first learnt classes are only based on a small X vector. The increasing of selected features maximizes the distance with previous learnt classes when a learnt class shares some new introduced descriptors. Fortunately, the system manages itself the relearning but introduces a delay in the network convergence and of course, more feedback from the user. Notice that 10% recall difference is 10% more rejection and hence, 10% more user feedbacks. In perspective, we plan to evaluate larger corpus to analyse this issue.

V. CONCLUSION AND FUTURE WORK

All these observations show the importance of the feature selection criteria. TF seems an interesting proposal because independent of other classes but not yet sufficient to filter unexpected terms. For instance generic terms shared by different classes are filtered by the IDF. The exploration of the criteria enhancement is a major perspective, like simulating the IDF or exploring the TF standard deviation.

The system was set-up for text vectors. However, our statistic approaches to discover a feature and embed it into A2ING is generic for any kind to feature which we can be observed within images. Our principle of a full incremental system for image classification could help computer vision and robotics to adapt to different progressive environments.

In conclusion we demonstrate both that we can have a full incremental efficient system, starting from scratch with really no prior knowledge and that an A2IGN can cope with a dynamic incremental feature vector. This system gives acceptable performance and several perspectives exist.

REFERENCES

[1] A. Joseph, "Automatic Detection of Fixed Expressions" PhD report, Université Paris 13, 2013

[2] A. Antonacopoulos, C. Clausner, C. Papadopoulos, and S. Pletschacher, "Icdar 2013 competition on historical newspaper layout analysis" IEEE International Conference on Document Analysis and Recognition, pp. 1454-1458, 2013

[3] A. Fornés, S. Escalera, J. Lladós, G. Sánchez, and J. Más, "Hand Drawn Symbol Recognition by Blurred Shape Model Descriptor and Multiclass Classifier" in "Graphics Recognition. Recent Advances and New Opportunities" Lecture Notes in Computer Science, vol.5046, pp. 30-40, Springer-Berlag, Berlin. 2008

[4] F. Alaei, N. Girard, S. Barrat, and JY. Ramel, "A New One-class Classification Method Based on Symbolic Representation: Application to Document Classification" 11th IAPR International Workshop on Document Analysis Systems, Tours, France, pp. 00-00, 2014

[5] F. Bouillot, "Text Classification: new weights adapted for small samples" PhD report, university of Montpellier, 2015

[6] H. Hamza, Y. Belaïd, A. Belaïd, and B. Baran Chaudhuri, "Incremental classification of invoice documents" 19th IEEE International Conference on Pattern Recognition (ICPR), Dec 2008, Tampa, United States, 2008

[7] K. Takeda, K. Kise, and M. Iwamura, "Real-Time Document Image Retrieval for a 10 Million Pages Database with a Memory Efficient andStability Improved LLAH" IEEE International Conference on Document Analysis and Recognition (ICDAR), Beijing, pp. 1054 - 1058, 2011

[8] M. Rusiñol, V. Poulain d'Andecy, D. Karatzas, and J. Llados, "Classification of Administrative Document Images by Logo Identification" GREC 2011, Seoul, Korea, Volume 7423 of the series Lecture Notes in Computer Science, pp. 49-58, 2011

[9] M-R. Bouguelia, "Classification and Active Learning from dynamic dataflows with incertain labels" PhD report, Université de Lorraine, 2015

[10] M-R. Bouguelia, Y. Belaïd, and A. Belaïd, "A stream-based semi-supervised active learning approach for document classification" IEEE International Conference on Document Analysis and Recognition (ICDAR), Washington DC (USA), pp. 611-615, August 2013

[11] N. Dalal and B. Triggs, "Histograms of oriented gradients for human detection" '05 Proceedings of the 2005 IEEE Computer Society Conference on Computer Vision and Pattern Recognition (CVPR'05), pp. 886-893, 2005

[12] P. Laskov, C. Gehl, K. Stefan, and K-R. Müller, 2006. "Incremental Support Vector Learning: Analysis, Implementation and Applications" J. Mach. Learn. Res. 7 (December 2006), pp. 1909-1936, 2006

[13] P. Sidiropoulos; S. Vrochidis; and I. Kompatsiaris. "Adaptive hierarchical density histogram for complex binary image retrieval" International workshop on Content-based Multimedia Indexing (CBMI), 2010

[14] R. Polikar, L. Upda, S. S. Upda, and V. Honavar. 2001. "Learn++: an incremental learning algorithm for supervised neural networks" Trans. Sys. Man Cyber Part C 31, 4, pp. 497-508, november 2001

[15] S. Chakraborty, N.K. Nagwani, and L. Dey. "Performance Comparison of Incremental K-means and Incremental DBSCAN Algorithms" International Journal of Computer Applications 27, pp. 14-18, August 2011

[16] S. Hamrouni, F. Cloppet, and N. Vincent, "Handwritten and printed text separation: linearity and regularity assessment" International Conference Image Analysis and Recognition, ICIAR14, Vilamoura, Portugal, pp. 387-394, 2014

[17] X. Zhang and Y. LeCun, "Text Understanding from Scratch" Technical Reports eprint arXiv : 1502.01710, february 2015

[18] X. Zhang, J. Zhao, and Y. LeCun, "Character-level Convolutional Networks for Text Classification" Advances in Neural Information Processing Systems 28 (NIPS), arXiv:1509.01626, december 2015

Enhanced Hash-based Intra Block Copy for HEVC Screen Content Coding using Sucessive Elimination Algorithm

Ilseung Kim
Department of Electronics and Computer Engineering
Hanyang University
Seoul, Korea
e-mail: ghanjang@gmail.com

Jechang Jeong
Department of Electronics and Computer Engineering
Hanyang University
Seoul, Korea
e-mail: jjeong@hanyang.ac.kr

Abstract—**An efficient algorithm is proposed not only to reduce the computation cost of the hash-based intra block copy (IBC), but also to achieve the Bjontegaard delta bit rate (BDBR) gain for High Efficiency Video Coding standard (HEVC) screen content coding(SCC). Recently, the HEVC Screen Content Coding Draft 6 was published including several new tools. Among those, hash-based intra block copy shows the high coding gain but it has a massive computational complexity even though it is adopted as a fast algorithm for global block search for IBC mode. The proposed algorithm suggests the effective way to calculate the lower bound for rate-distortion (RD) cost when performing the hash-based IBC process and to eliminate the impossible candidates earlier. Experimental results show that about 50% on the average and up to 86.80% of the search points can be early terminated as well as 0.21% on the average BDBR saving can be achieved compared to HM-16.8+SCM-6.1.**

Keywords; HEVC; Screen content coding(scc); Intra Block copy(IBC); Hash.

I. INTRODUCTION

High Efficiency Video Coding standard (HEVC) [1] is the most recent international video coding standard jointly developed by Joint Collaborative Team on Video Coding (JCT-VC) and it was finalized in January 2013. HEVC is able to achieve around 50% bit-rate reduction under the equivalent subjective visual quality circumstances, compared with H.264/MPEG-4 AVC standard [2][3].

Recently, on the other hand, there has been a proliferation of applications which utilize the computer generated contents, such as wireless display, remote desktop, external display interfacing, and cloud computing, etc. [4]. However, the type of video content used in these applications has different characteristics compared with that of the camera-captured content, such as containing no sensor noise, having large uniformly flat areas, repeated patterns, and a limited number of different colors and so on.

Even though there are several sequences that contain screen contents in the common test sequences, such as Class F, HEVC may not be efficient for the sequences whose characteristics are different from the camera-captured natural video contents because it was developed with a main focus on dealing with camera-captured natural video contents. Accordingly, there have been requirements for coding of screen content. In order to reflect these requirements, the MPEG Requirements subgroup published a set of requirements for an extension of HEVC for coding of screen content in January 2014 [4] and currently the HEVC Screen Content Coding (SCC) Draft 6 was published in February 2016 [5][6].

In HEVC-SCC, 4 major techniques/tools have been introduced: Palette mode, Adaptive colour transform (ACT), Adaptive motion vector resolution, and Intra block copy (IBC). Palette mode utilizes the observation that a number of different colour value frequently exist for screen content. A lot of HEVC-SCC test materials consist of RGB colour format or YCbCr 4:4:4 format, whose inter-colour component correlation is very high. In order to remove inter-colour component redundancy, ACT has been introduced in SCC. Unlike camera captured content, there is no need to use fractional motion compensation for much screen content. For this reason, adaptive motion vector has adopted in SCC. There are a lot of repeated patterns such as characters in screen content, so the motion estimation and compensation within the current picture can be effective. IBC is the technique that conducts the motion estimation and compensation within the current picture as shown in Fig. 1.

In HEVC-SCC Draft 6, there are two kinds of block vector search method for IBC: local search mode and global search mode and hash-based block vector search technique has been adopted for global search mode. This paper provides an overview of technical issues of IBC and presents a tool for improving IBC, especially hash-based block vector search.

Figure 1. An example of IBC from sc_map video sequence

This paper is organized as follows: Section II describes a technical features of IBC as a conventional algorithm. Section III presents the proposed algorithm. Section IV discusses the experiment results and the conclusion is set forth in Section V.

II. Intra Block Copy (IBC) in HEVC-SCC Draft 6

Basically, IBC is the technique that conducts the motion estimation (ME) and compensation within the current picture. Block matching is performed in order to find the optimal block vector and to calculate the lowest rate-distortion (RD) cost like ME but within a current picture. On the other hand, there are two kinds of IBC modes in SCC: local block vector search and global block vector search for IBC mode. In SCC, a local area search is performed first and a global search is followed. Comparing RD cost from both search, choose the block vector with the minimum RD cost.

A. *Local block vector search for IBC mode*

In this step, there are two steps find the optimal block vectors (BVs). First, find the four best BVs according to their RD cost, where

$$RD\_cost = SAD_{luma} + \lambda \times BV_{bits} \tag{1}$$

within 2 CTU for the local search as depicted in Fig. 2 where BV_{bits} is the number of bits needed to signal the BV. In this step, only the SAD of the luma component is used. For the chosen four best BVs, additional RD cost is calculated as

$$RD\_cost = SAD_{luma} + SAD_{chroma} + \lambda \times BV_{bits} \tag{2}$$

, in order to find the locally optimal block vector BV_{opt}^{local}. The RD cost corresponding to BV_{opt}^{local} is denoted by $RD\_cost_{opt}^{local}$.

B. *Global block vector search for IBC mode*

Global block vector search is conducted for 8x8 and 16x16 blocks. As shown in Fig. 3, the entire reconstructed current picture before loop filtering is the global search prediction area. For 16x16 blocks, a one-dimensional search is performed over the entire reconstructed current picture, as shown in Fig. 4. For the horizontal search, block matching is performed only in the horizontal direction that means vertical components of BVs are zero with the same height of the current block and the vertical search is performed in the same manner.

For 8x8 PUs, a hash-based full picture search is used to search the optimal BV. The 16-bit hash entries for the current block and the reference block are calculated using the original sample values. Let Grad denote the gradient of the 8x8 block and let dc0, dc1, dc2, and dc3 denote the DC values of the four 4x4 sub-blocks of the 8x8 block. Then, the 16-bit hash entry H is calculated as:

$$H = MSB(dc0,3) << 13 + MSB(dc1,3) << 10 + MSB(dc2,3) << 7 + MSB(dc2,3) << 4 + MSB(Grad,4), \tag{3}$$

where MSB(X,n) represents the n most significant bits of X.

The procedure of hash-based IBC is as follows: First, the hash-value of the current PU is calculated. Search the blocks which have the same hash value with the current PU in the pre-calculated hash list. Then, the blocks that have the same hash value with that of the current block perform the RD cost and choose the eight best BVs according to (1). For the chosen eight best BVs, additional RD cost is calculated using (2) in order to find the BV_{opt}^{global}.

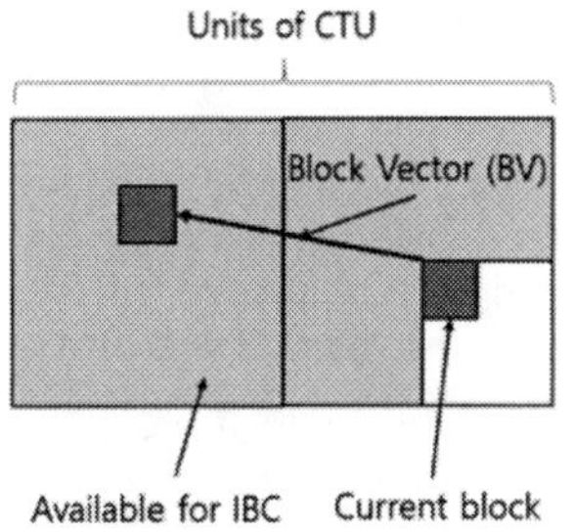

Figure 2. Local block vector search prediction area

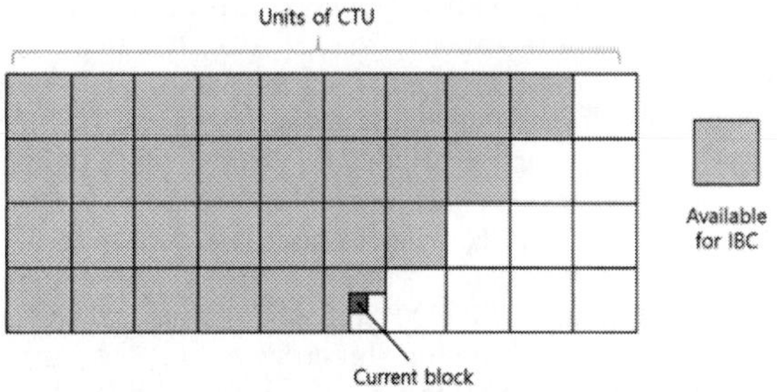

Figure 3. Global block vector search prediction area

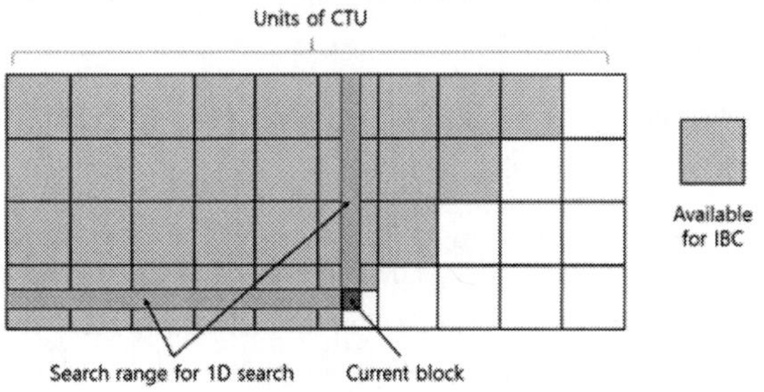

Figure 4. A one-dimensional search prediction area for 16x16 blocks

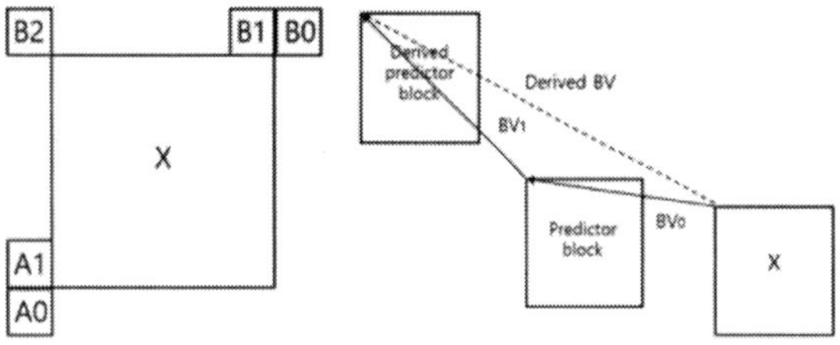

(a) Spatial BV predictors (B) Derived BV predictors

Figure 5. IBC prediction area

C. *Fast block vector search for IBC mode*

If the residual of inter prediction is not zero, some fast search and early termination methods are employed, between evaluating the RD cost of inter mode and intra mode. It is applied only to 2Nx2N partition of various CU sizes. If the residue of fast IBC search is not zero, then regular intra mode will be performed as described in Sections A and B.

The SAD-based RD costs of using a set of BV predictors are calculated in the fast search. As shown in Fig. 5, the set includes the five spatial neighboring BV as used in inter merge mode and the last two coded BVs. In addition, the derived BVs of the block pointed to by each of the aforementioned BV predictors are also included.

III. PROPOSED ALGORITHM

Hash-based IBC mode for the 8x8 PU has a critical role in SCC. Compared with SCC without hash-based IBC, up to 75% Bjøntegaard Distortion bitrate (BD-BR) gain can be achieved. On the other hand, even though the main purpose of using hash-based search is to speed up the full picture search, it has a massive computation burden when there are a number of blocks in the hash list. For example, over 70 thousand times RD cost calculations are performed on the average for 8x8 PU, when we encode "sc_wordEditing_1280x720_8bit_444" sequence under the intra_main_SCC condition. In order to alleviate this, we apply the concept of the successive elimination algorithm (SEA) [7] for the 8x8 PUs which are used for hash-based search.

The derivation of the SEA starts from the following basic triangular inequalities,

$$\begin{cases} f_c(i,j) - f_r(i-x, j-y) \le \left| f_c(i,j) - f_r(i-x, j-y) \right| \\ f_r(i-x, j-y) - f_c(i,j) \le \left| f_c(i,j) - f_r(i-x, j-y) \right| \end{cases}, \quad (4)$$

where $f_c(i,j)$ and $f_r(i,j)$ denote the intensity of the pixel with coordinate (i,j) in the current picture and the reference picture, (x,y) represents the displacement of the BVs, respectively.

By using (4), it can be easily shown that the following relation holds:

$$\begin{aligned} &\left| \sum_{i,j=0}^{N} f_c(i,j) - \sum_{i,j=0}^{N} f_r(i-x, j-y) \right| \\ &\le \sum_{i,j=0}^{N} \left| f_c(i,j) - f_r(i-x^*, j-y^*) \right| = SAD(x^*, y^*), \end{aligned} \quad (5)$$

where (x^*, y^*) denotes the displacement of the optimal BV. This means that the difference of the sum norms of the current block and the reference block cannot exceed the SAD value of the search point, so we can distinguish the impossible candidate using the sum norms and SAD value. In this case, $SAD(x^*, y^*)$ and (x^*, y^*) can be updated by $SAD(x, y)$ and (x, y), respectively, if $SAD(x, y)$ is less than $SAD(x^*, y^*)$. Also, applying (5) into (1), then it can be easily demonstrated the following inequality:

$$\begin{aligned} &\left| \sum_{i,j=0}^{N} f_c(i,j) - \sum_{i,j=0}^{N} f_r(i-x, j-y) \right| + \lambda \times BV_{bits} \\ &\le RD\_cost_{min}. \end{aligned} \quad (6)$$

Note that all the procedure of the proposed algorithm is applied when the hash value is matched. The procedure of the proposed algorithm is as follows: Calculate the $\lambda \times BV_{bits}$ first and then check (6) with the sum norms and the value of RD_cost_{min}. If the condition does not hold, discard the search point and move on to next search point. Once the search point is skipped, that point cannot be included as a candidate set aforementioned in Section II. C.

Note that the sum norm for each block has been already calculated when calculating the 16-bit hash entry H in (3). In other words, there is no additional computation to get the sum norms of the current block and reference blocks.

IV. EXPERIMENT RESULTS

In order to demonstrate the coding efficiency of the proposed algorithm, we simulated five sequences in the common test conditions (CTC) used during the development of HEVC-SCC [8] and a sequence from the HEVC CTC in Class F as listed in Table I under the intra_main_scc configuration condition. HM-16.8+SCM-6.1 was modified to include the proposed algorithm. 22, 27, 32, and 37 are set for QPs.

TABLE I. TEST SEQUENCES

Resolution	Sequence name	YCbCr color format
1920x1080	sc_desktop_1920x1080_60_8bit	4:4:4
1920x1080	MissionControlClip3_1920x1080_60_8b444	4:4:4
1280x720	sc_web_browsing_1280x720_30_8bit	4:4:4
1280x720	sc_map_1280x720_30_8bit	4:4:4
1280x720	sc_wordEditing_1280x720_30_8bit	4:4:4
1280x720	slideEditing_1280x720_30	4:2:0

TABLE II. PERFORMANCE COMPARISON BETWEEN HM-16.8 AND HM-16.8+SCM-6.1.

Sequence name	BD-BR (%)
sc_desktop_1920x1080_60_8bit	-84.01
MissionControlClip3_1920x1080_60_8b444	-28.24
sc_web_browsing_1280x720_30_8bit	-51.32
sc_map_1280x720_30_8bit	-80.88
sc_wordEditing_1280x720_30_8bit	-68.54
slideEditing_1280x720_30	-48.50
Average	-60.25

TABLE III. PERFORMANCE COMPARISON WITH VERSUS WITHOUT HASH-BASED IBC FOR HM-16.8+SCM-6.1.

Sequence name	BD-BR (%)
sc_desktop_1920x1080_60_8bit	-75.56
MissionControlClip3_1920x1080_60_8b444	-4.12
sc_web_browsing_1280x720_30_8bit	-27.00
sc_map_1280x720_30_8bit	-67.90
sc_wordEditing_1280x720_30_8bit	-54.19
slideEditing_1280x720_30	-21.54
Average	-41.72

TABLE IV. PERFORMANCE COMPARISON BETWEEN HM-16.8+SCM-6.1 AND THE PROPOSED ALGORITHM.

Sequence name	BD-BR (%)
sc_desktop_1920x1080_60_8bit	-0.62
MissionControlClip3_1920x1080_60_8b444	0.00
sc_web_browsing_1280x720_30_8bit	-0.13
sc_map_1280x720_30_8bit	-0.26
sc_wordEditing_1280x720_30_8bit	-0.22
slideEditing_1280x720_30	0.00
Average	-0.21

TABLE V. EARLY TERMINATION RATIO COMPARED TO HM-16.8+SCM-6.1 (%)

Sequence name	Ratio (%)
sc_desktop_1920x1080_60_8bit	57.25
MissionControlClip3_1920x1080_60_8b444	26.40
sc_web_browsing_1280x720_30_8bit	86.80
sc_map_1280x720_30_8bit	42.55
sc_wordEditing_1280x720_30_8bit	45.50
slideEditing_1280x720_30	35.43
Average	48.99

Table II shows the bit-rate savings SCC tools over HM-16.8 for intra main configuration. Note that negative number indicates the BD-BR saving. BD-BR savings in the range of 28.24% to 84.01% and 60.25% on the average can be observed.

Aforementioned in Section III, hash-based global IBC search has an important role in SCC as shown in Table III. Except some sequences like "MissionControlClip3", BDBR saving rate is quite high; about 40% BDBR saving can be observed.

Table IV shows the performance comparison between HM-16.8+SCM-6.1 and the proposed algorithm. Even though we proposed a kind of an early termination methods over hash-based IBC, we can achieve the BDBR saving up to 0.62% and 0.21% on the average. The interesting point is that the sequences which have the higher coding gain by using hash-based IBC also have the higher coding gain for the proposed algorithm. We can obtain the coding gain by eliminating the impossible search points that may be a bad influence on BV predictors from as a candidate set aforementioned in Section II. C.

It is demonstrated that the impossible search point can be effectively removed by checking (6) as shown in Table V. The impossible candidates are removed up to 86.80% and about 50% on the average.

V. CONCLUSION

In this paper, enhanced hash-based intra block copy algorithm using successive elimination algorithm is proposed, after analyzing the conventional IBC technique in HEVC SCC Draft 6, especially hash-based IBC. The proposed algorithm suggests the efficient way to calculate the lower bound for RD cost when performing the hash-based IBC process and to eliminate the impossible candidates earlier. Experimental results show that about 50% on the average and up to 86.80% of the search points can be early terminated as well as 0.21% on the average BDBR saving can be achieved compared to HM-16.8+SCM-6.1.

ACKNOWLEDGMENT

"This research was supported by Basic Science Research Program through the National Research Foundation of Korea(NRF) funded by the Ministry of Science, ICT and future Planning(NRF-2015R1A2A2A01006004)"

REFERENCES

[1] G. J. Sullivan, J. Ohm, W.-J. Han, and T. Wiegand, "Overview of the High Efficiency Video Coding (HEVC) Standard," *IEEE Trans. Circuits Syst. Video Technol.*, vol. 22, no. 12, pp. 1649-1668, Dec. 2012

[2] J. Ohm, G. J. Sullivan, H. Schwarz, T. Tan, and T. Wiegand " Comparison of the coding efficiency of video coding standards – including High Efficiency Video Coding (HEVC)," *IEEE Trans. Circuits Syst. Video Technol.*, vol. 22, no. 12, pp. 1669–1684, Dec. 2012.

[3] Advanced Video Coding for Generic Audiovisual Services, ITU-T and ISO/IEC JTC1, document ITU-T Rec. H.264 and ISO/IEC 14496-10, May 2003.

[4] H. Yu, K. McCann, R. Cohen, and P. Amon, Requirements for an Extension of HEVC for Coding of Screen Content, ISO/IEC JTC

1/SC 29/WG 11, document MPEG2014/N14174, San Jose, CA, USA, Jan. 2014.

[5] R. Joshi. et. al., "HEVC Screen Content Coding Draft Text 6," 23rd JCT-VC meeting, San Diego, U.S. document JCTVC-W1005, Feb. 2016.

[6] R. Joshi, J. Xu, R. Cohen, S. Liu, and Y. Ye, "Screen content coding test model 6 (SCM 6)," 22nd JCT-VC meeting, Geneva, Switzerland, document JCTVC-V1014, Oct. 2015.

[7] W. Li and E. Salari, "Successive elimination algorithm for motion estimation," IEEE Trans. Image Process., vol. 8, pp. 105-107, Jan. 1995.

[8] H. Yu, R. Cohen, K. Rapaka, and J. Xu, " Common test coditions for screen content coding," 20th JCT-VC meeting, Geneva, Switzerland, document JCT-VC-T1005, Feb. 2015.

Research on Optimization Technology of Three Dimensional Model

Jing Zhang
College of Computer Science and Technology,
Harbin Engineering University,
Harbin, Heilongjiang, China
e-mail: zhangjing@hrbeu.edu.cn

Bowen Li
College of Computer Science and Technology,
Harbin Engineering University,
Harbin, Heilongjiang, China
e-mail: libowen@hrbeu.edu.cn

Tianchi Zhang
College of Computer Science and Technology,
Harbin Engineering University,
Harbin, Heilongjiang, China
e-mail: zhangtianchi@hrbeu.edu.cn

***Abstract*—Method of reconstruction and model simplification are two key optimization technologies for three dimensional model, there are several problems in these methods, such as, low time consume, bad interface and accuracy problem. Firstly, existing methods and implementation toolkits related with our research are introduced. Secondly, a modified reconstruction algorithm based on Voronoi diagram is proposed. Thirdly, a new algorithm of semi-automatic mesh simplification is presented with the aim of simplifying error correction and achieving higher efficiency. Finally, two tests are implemented to prove that our new methods can improve the efficiency of reconstruction and has a good visualization performance.**

Keywords—Three Dimensional Model; Optimization Technology; Reconstruction; Mesh simplification

I. INTRODUCTION

With the development of image processing technology and laser scanning technology, 3D reconstruction technology has become an important research content for a wide range of applications in the field of reverse engineering, pattern recognition, film and television, and obtained the rapid development. The complex model is constructed quickly and accurately through the 3D point data. The existing reconstruction algorithms are mainly divided into two main categories: volume reconstruction and surface reconstruction [1]. Volume reconstruction needs a long execution time to be processed. Surface reconstruction processing speed is relatively fast, and it is good for real-time processing. Surface reconstruction mainly includes three phases: contour line connection, contour extraction and triangulation. Contour line connection means connecting the adjacent cross section contour points. Contour extraction is a virtual cube formed by the eight neighbouring points, which represent the contour surface of a polygon. Triangulation is a construction of tetrahedral mesh. The higher the processing speed of surface reconstruction, the lower accuracy it has, because of the lack of some contour points. For this reason, we propose a 3D data reconstruction algorithm based on improving Voronoi diagram in which the 3D point data is filtered and de-noise.

The details of our research are as follows. In Section II, we introduce the critical technologies related with our research, including 3D visualization class library Visualization Toolkit (VTK), Voronoi diagram reconstruction method and semi-automated mesh simplification method. In Section III, our new method realization is presented, including realization of new construction method and Semi-automatic simplification method. There are two tests in Section IV, the first test is used to prove that our surface reconstruction method is feasible and efficient, the second test is to confirm that our method of semi-automatic mesh simplification has good interface and is accurate. In Section V, we present a conclusion about our research.

II. CRITICAL TECHNOLOGIES

In this section, we introduce critical technologies related with our research, including 3D visualization class library VTK, reconstruction method and semi-automated mesh simplification method.

A. 3D visualization class library VTK

In 3D visualization class library VTK, there are three key parts: Voronoi tessellation code, Vanderpool (VT) and VTK. Voronoi tessellation code defines a cellular-like structure, where each particle is associated to a region in which any point in that region is nearer to that particle than to any other particle. The parallel Voronoi tessellation code is an open source code, and it has the following characteristics: (1) parallel and optimization, has full advantage of actual multicore and distributed memory, (2) user-friendly in documentation and interface, (3) has typical I/O formats used in the field of NN-body simulations. In addition, this code also has the properties such as Voronoi densities, cell volumes, density gradients, and immediate neighbour lists. In the field of astrophysics, particularly for NN-body simulations, Voronoi tessellation code is a very useful tool to identify immediate neighbours of particles, and it is one of the best adaptive methods to recover a precise density field from a discrete distribution of points, with a clear advantage over smoothed particle hydrodynamic or other interpolation-based techniques. Its principal asset is complete independence of arbitrary smoothing functions and parameters specifying their properties.

Vanderpool (VT) in 3D visualization reproduces the anisotropies of the local particle distribution and through its adaptive and local nature proves to be optimally suited for uncovering the full structural richness in the density distribution. Other remarkable uses of VT in this field are filamentary structure identification, NN-body simulation code AREPO, halo and void identification, and nonparametric determination of halo concentrations.

In 3D visualization class library, VTK is a set of 3D graphics, image processing and visualization tools which is integrated with the C++ library developed by the United States Kitware company. It is a source development, visualization technology and image processing software system; it can be used in C++, TCL/TK, Java and Python language environments [2]. It combines computer graphics, image processing and visualization technology, and it has an absolute advantage in the field of visualization and image processing. It has become often used in the research of image visualization system. VTK system mainly has two kinds: the graphic model object and visualization object model. The main function of graphical model is representing the scene which is formed from geometry by graph. VTK has 3D interactive components where users can choose the functions of parallel processing, running algorithm and visualization process. Visualization process includes functions of read data, filtering, mapping and rendering.

B. *The method of Voronoi diagram reconstruction*

The accuracy and efficiency are two key factors of 3D surface reconstruction by data. The accuracy is required to maintain the topology and shape. The efficiency is required to reduce the reconstruction time in the premise of maintaining the original topology under. Distance algorithm deals with noisy scattered data and it also reconstructs the surface of triangular mesh concerning for sample density and surface details based on a greedy filter.

The original Voronoi diagram [3] has a great effect on the distance between the point and other geometric objects. Assuming that in a given plane or space, there are n scattered points, point set $P = \{p_1, p_2, \ldots\ldots, p_n\}$, defined as:

$$V(\mathrm{p}_i) = \bigcap_{j \neq i} H_i(p_i, p_j) \tag{1}$$

$$H(p_i, p_j) = \{d(p, p_i) < d(p, p_j), i \neq j, p_i, p_j \in P\} \tag{2}$$

Among them, $H(p_i, p_j)$ indicated the trajectory formed from the points. The distance between them and p_i is closer than the distance between them and p_j and the trajectory is either 1.5 or 1.5 spaces. $d(p, p_i)$ is Euclidean distance between p and p_i. $V(\mathrm{p}_i)$ is sum of trajectories from p_j to p_i. There is a Voronoi polygon corresponding to each point in the point set P, the sum of all the polygons called the Voronoi diagram of point set P.

Delaunay triangulation is dual related to Voronoi diagram, which has the characteristics of the maximum of the minimum angle, the cavity and the local reconnection [4]. Power map is an extension of Voronoi; its generating element can be regarded as the Voronoi figure of the Power circle, and the distance is not Euclidean distance but Power distance:

The known D dimensional point set S, the weight of $p \in S$ is $w_p (-\infty < w_p < +\infty)$ and there is:

$$\pi_p(x) = \|x - p\|^2 - w_p \tag{3}$$

$\pi_p(x)$ is Power distance of x to p. Power graph and its dual regular triangulation are corresponding to weighted points of Voronoi graph and Delaunay triangulation.

If we hope to obtain better approximation of the surface vector of sampling point, we need to improve the surface reconstruction algorithm. The details of our improved method are described in Section III A.

C. *Semi-automated mesh simplification method*

For regular models, such as airplane, tank, etc., model conforms to a certain rule, automatic error correction can be easily achieved by feature preserving simplification [5]. However, for the cows, dinosaurs and other irregular model, or users who have special expectations to simplify models, we need select error correction mode and the expected characteristics of the region are preserved.

The basic error measure is quadric error metrics, which focuses on the feature of size in shape variable before and after the simplification. In many cases, the curvature of the model is more important than the feature ones. For surfaces that are in the same plane, only a few polygons can be expressed, however highly curved surfaces require more polygons to represent [6]. For this reason, we study the curvature error and the two-error weight as the result of automatic error correction, and do research on the triangle optimization factor to the quality of triangle.

The three vertices of the triangle V3, V2 and V1 are used to calculate the product of vectors, which are the normal vectors of triangle:

$$normal = \begin{bmatrix} v_{x1} - v_{x2} \\ v_{y1} - v_{y2} \\ v_{z1} - v_{z2} \end{bmatrix} \times \begin{bmatrix} v_{x2} - v_{x3} \\ v_{y2} - v_{y3} \\ v_{z2} - v_{z3} \end{bmatrix} \quad (4)$$

The curvature error metric of the edge (u, v) after the folding is

$$F(u,v) = Len(u,v) \times Cur(uv) \quad (5)$$

$Len(u,v)$ represents the length of the edge (u,v), $Cur(uv)$ represents the curvature of the edge (u, v). In order to find the longest distant u adjacent to the triangle from the other triangle, we compare the value of the curvature from the collapsed edge (u, v) of the two surface normal point product.

If a triangle is closer to the equilateral triangle, it is regular [7]. Triangle optimization is to avoid appearing long and narrow triangles in the simplified process [8]-[12]. It tries to make the generated triangle approaches in an equilateral triangle.

Set in T_i , there are three generation of triangle edges l_1 , l_2 and l_3 , when the T_i triangle is an equilateral triangle, then, $\frac{(l_1 + l_2 - l_3)}{l_2} = 1$ .If the shape of the triangle is longer, the value of $\frac{(l_1 + l_2 - l_3)}{l_2}$ is closer to 0. The value of $\frac{(l_1 + l_2 - l_3)}{2 \times l_2}$ is always in (0,1). So in this paper the definition of regular triangle P is:

$$\mathrm{Re}(P) = \frac{(l_1 + l_2 - l_3)}{l_2} \quad (6)$$

In order to improve the result of the simplification, users can mark in 3D model to refine and retain in the simplified platform directly, and simplify to achieve new simplified results. The user impact factor of the marked area is embodied in the way of weight. In our new error method, we set weight value of W both by system initialization and by calculation of each point. The initialization value of W is 1. If the user did not make any other decision, the way of automatic error correction will be followed. If the user tag, the tag area will be given a new weight, and the value of W > 1, the twice error will be modified by following formula:

$$\Delta'(u,v) = w_v \Delta(u) + w_v \Delta(v) \quad (7)$$

The error is multiplied twice by a weight. To calculate the initial value of weight, we provide two methods to set the initial weights in the system; the details are presented in Section III B.

III. REALIZATION OF OUR NEW METHODS

There are two improved methods in this section; one improved method is to improve Power Crust Algorithm, other improved method is semi-automatic mesh simplification method.

A. The concrete realization of Power Crust

Power Crust algorithm has the advantages of a simple process to accurately reconstruct the results, for a large number of scattered point cloud data without a normal vector [13]-[14]. The processing speed is very fast, but the disadvantage of this method is that it is not accurate [15]. Power Crust algorithm can generate a watertight and sealed 3D mesh; in addition, it can construct the estimators from the central axis of the original surface which contains noise, sharp and unclosed points cloud data. The steps of Power Crust algorithm are:

- Calculate centre axis of the sample, find out v vertices to create graph on Voronoi triangulation ,
- Connect through triangulation points of the original point cloud into triangular mesh model,
- Delete the grid which does not comply with requirements.
- Construction of the grid mesh

The advantage of Power Crust algorithm is that it can construct the region with dense points. Its disadvantage is that the output of discrete surface has sparse points. We modify Power Crust algorithm based on Voronoi diagram:

1) Set Delaunay triangulation by sampling point S; and find the Voronoi vertex which the boundary box of vertex is considered to be the sampling point in Power diagram.

2) Determine which Voronoi vertices are poles.

3) The generation of the pole penalty set Bp, calculated the Power chart.

4) Mark each pole inside or outside.

5) Set the triangle as the output, and return the results.

We would prove that our modified algorithm has better result by experiments in Section IV.

B. Modified Semi- automatic mesh simplification method

There are two methods to set weight value in mesh simplification method; in the first method, users input a weight value, the second method consists on setting an initial weight value by the system, because it may be difficult for some users and cases to actually set suitable weights. For different grid model, weights will have great differences.

The two methods of set weight value are: 1) User input weight value to system. This method can meet user different requirements. The weight values include maximum and minimum values. 2) Initial label the mean value of the error in the actual simplification process for different mesh models. If the pre-set weight range is large, it is likely that role to the quadric error led to final folding.

We modify semi-automatic mesh simplification method by calculating the weight value two times so that the error would not make model losing retention effect. Model when it is in the medium errors are in reasonable way because that model retention effect is better than at other errors .The twice error and the weight of the transfer process are done separately. The definition of weight transfer is as follows:

1) The process of Edge collapse: Point v_1 and v_2 fold to v .The weight value of v_1 is w_1, weight value of v_2 is w_2. Weight value of v is average value of w_1 and w_2.

2) The process of Split point process: The parent node V is split into two nodes, if v weight is w, then two sub-node weights are w.

The semi-automatic mesh simplification code is described as follows:

1) E(u,v):=v.quadric/v.opt+F(u,v);
2) W(u,v):=(u.weight+v.weight)/2;
3) Cost(u,v):=W(u)*E(u)+W(v)*E(v);
4) Mesh.list.sort(mesh.v,cost(u,v));
5) Mesh.list.popfront();
6) Mesh.update();
7) If is Ok (mesh) then
8) return mesh;
9) else goto step5;
10) end if

The algorithm needs to deal with a large amount of data, so the definition of a suitable data structure ensures simplification and the capability of handling large data models quickly. The modified semi-automatic mesh simplification is as follows:

1) Set sequence of vertices, which record each vertex and adjacency edge, adjacent triangles, error values and weights.

2) Record vertex triangle index sequence.

3) Identify the sequence of vertices and triangles sequence model data structure.

4) Store the folded edge in the record list.

The modified algorithm will be tested and analysed by experiments in section IV.

IV. EXPERIMENT AND ANALYSIS

There are two tests in this section; one test is a reconstruction test aiming at proving our improved algorithm of reconstruction described in section III A; the second test is to verify our improved algorithm of semi-automatic mesh simplification method being described in section III B. The data used in experiment came from the 3D scanned images stored in the Txt text [16] in the form of 3D coordinates.

A. Reconstruction test and analysis

The program of surface reconstruction and visualization in 3D point cloud are designed based on Visual C++ Microsoft platform. We choose two sets of three dimensional point cloud data, such as data of whale and ocean to do the tests. They are shown in Figure 1 and Figure 2.

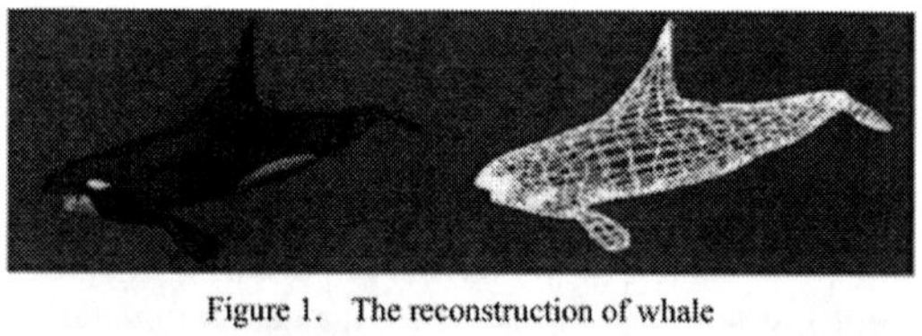

Figure 1. The reconstruction of whale

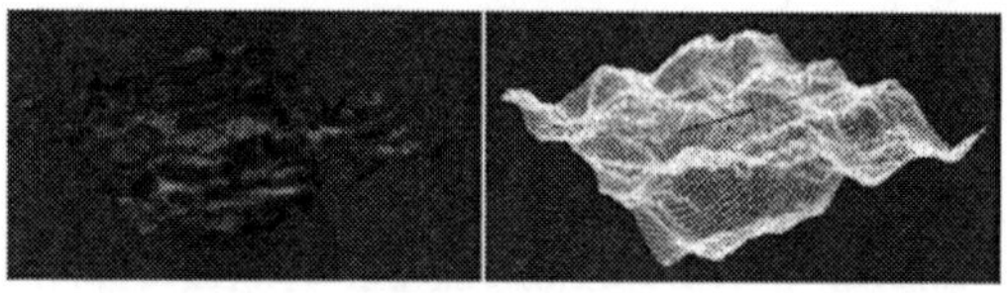

Figure 2. The reconstruction of ocean

We achieve two reconstruction effects both by using Crust Power algorithm through the 3D point cloud data and by using our algorithm through the 3D point cloud data to carry out a comparative analysis. Table 1 summarizes the results of the reconstruction of the two algorithms.

TABLE I. TWO METHODS OF SURFACE RECONSTRUCTION OF DIFFERENT POINT CLOUD MODEL

Point cloud data	Number of point	Power Crust Time/s	Our method time/s
Whale	5000	6.03	3.52
Ocean	20000	15.36	10.27

Through the above tests, we can find that the time efficiency of power crust algorithm is lower than our method. Our reconstruction method based on Voronoi diagram can achieve the stereo effect of 3D point cloud well and can retain some details of the original object. Therefore, our reconstruction method based on Voronoi diagram is an effective method in surface reconstruction.

B. Experiment and analysis of semi-automatic mesh simplification method

Our semi-automatic mesh simplification method was implemented by the standard C++ language. There are several parts in this program, such as error correction, edit mode, different simplified models and default settings.

User error correction for weight allows the users to do marking operation. In edit mode, the user can alter attention region (the region should be distinguished by different colors) which facilitate the user operation through CTRL + mouse to select smear colour; SHIFT + mouse to delete the selected colour. For different simplified models, the range of calculation errors and the ranking results are different. The weight of the error is proposed to properly affect the calculation of the results of the calculation error, and therefore, the appropriate value of the initial weight is the key influence on error calculation. According to the different weights of the experimental model, the optimal setting is to obtain the minimum and maximum error, and then take the average value between the two values as the initial value for the corresponding model. The default settings for the user's marking area are the initial value and the value of the tag. Specific weights are set shown in Table II.

TABLE II. THE INITIAL WEIGHTS OF THE TWO MODELS.

model	Minimum error	Maximum error	Initial weight	Mark weight
whale	0.0	0.38589	0.194735	0.287543
Ocean	0.0	0.78723	0.287543	0.589832

The results of our method to achieve the 3D model of simplification are shown in Figure 3, Figure 4 and Figure 5. According to the initial weight of the set rules, the weights are the average between the initial weight and the maximum error.

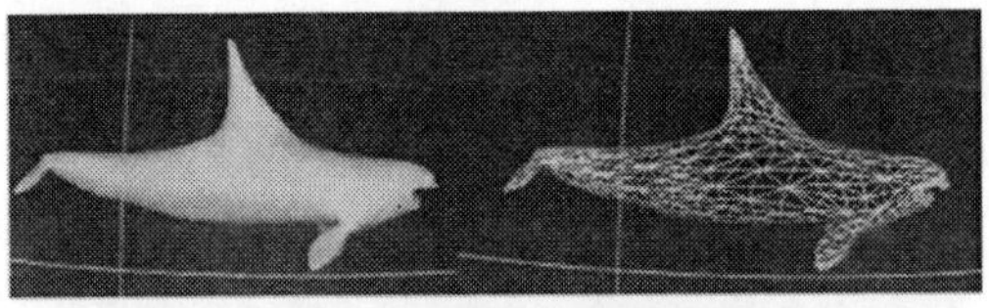

Figure 3. The initial model of whale

Figure 4. Reduced to 60% of whale

Figure 5. Reduced to 40% of whale

The result of simplification of ocean model by our method is shown in Figure 6, Figure 7 and Figure 8.

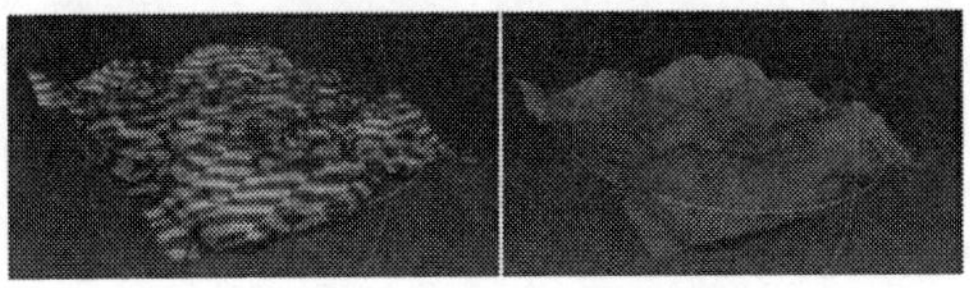

Figure 6. The initial model of ocean

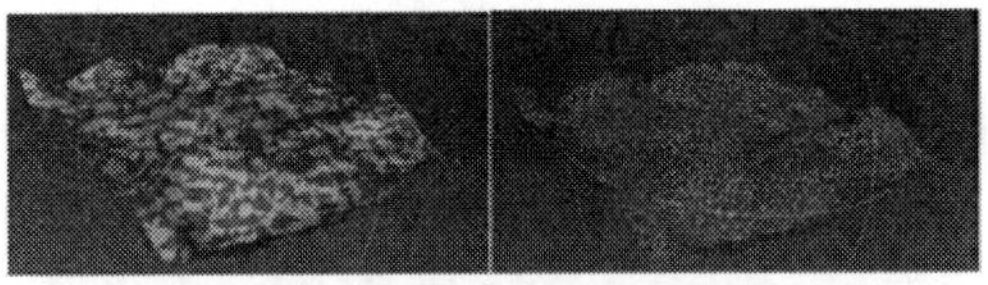

Figure 7. Reduced to 60% of ocean

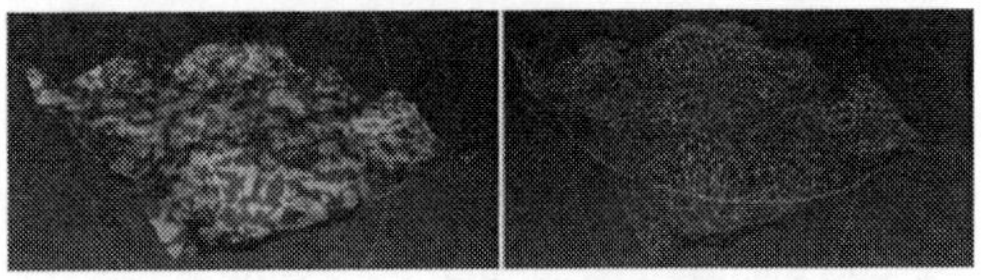

Figure 8. Reduced to 40% of ocean

We use the function of user error correction to get the best simplification result. Labelled and unlabelled mesh simplification results are shown in Table III.

TABLE III. THE NUMBER OF MESH MODEL SIMPLIFICATION RESULTS.

Simplification degree	Whole area	Marked area	Unlabeled area
Original model	2645	568	2077
60% of whale model	1587	738	849
40% of whale model	1058	539	519

From the experiment results, we conclude that our semi- automatic mesh simplification algorithm can obtain the simplified model conforms to the simplified criteria. It can also fully retain the local area which users concern about maintaining the appearance. It can be seen that our modified algorithm is important in generating a simplified model and it is consistent with user's requirements.

V. CONCLUSION

In this paper, we firstly analyse the existing surface reconstruction of Voronoi and Delaunay triangulation Power Crust algorithms and study the implementation toolkit of VTK. Secondly, we modified Power Crust algorithm based on Voronoi diagram to reconstruct the surface by using the cloud data into VTK which has a strong image processing capabilities. Our modified method can effectively improve the efficiency of reconstruction and has a good visualization performance. Thirdly, based on the two error metric algorithm, we proposed a new method of semi-automatic mesh simplification. Our algorithm provides automatic error correction and user error correction which has twice error correction functions according to different models with different types of error correction. By comparing with different models obtained by different experiments, our semi-automatic mesh simplification method has the characteristics of good retention effect and can simplify the complex structure of the model.

ACKNOWLEDGEMENT

This research is supported by (1) 2017-2020 The National Natural Science Fund (Project No.51679058). (2) 2013-2016 China Higher Specialized Research Fund (PhD supervisor category) (20132304110018).

REFERENCES

[1] T. Pincell, V. Petrov, G. Brajnik, R. Ciprian, and V. Lollobrigida, Design and optimization of a modular setup for measurements of three-dimensional spin polarization with ultrafast pulsed sources. Scientific Instruments 87(3). pp. 5146-570, 2016.

[2] L. Wei, L. Y. Ju, and C. H. Lin, Research on Three-Dimensional Reconstruction Technology Based on the Data of Hybrid Measurement. Advanced Materials Research 1039. pp. 30-35, 2014.

[3] D. Hirpa, W. Hare, Y. Lucet, Y. Pushak, and S. Tesfamariam, A bi-objective optimization framework for three-dimensional road alignment design. Transportation Research Part C Emerging Technologies 65. pp. 61-78, 2016.

[4] Kurata, Yasuhisa, Optimization of non-contrast-enhanced MR angiography of the renal artery with three-dimensional balanced steady-state free-precession and time-spatial labeling inversion pulse (time-SLIP) at 3T MRI, in relation to age and blood velocity. Abdominal radiology41(1). pp. 1-8, 2015.

[5] Y. YueTzu, T. HsiangWen, and J. ShihJie, Numerical simulation and optimization of turbulent nanofluids in a three-dimensional wavy channel. Numerical Heat Transfer Applications 69. pp. 1-17, 2016.

[6] Q. Wang, H. Zhang, H. Cai, Q. Fan, and G. Li, Reconstruction of co-continuous ceramic composites three-dimensional microstructure solid model by generation-based optimization method. Computational Materials Science117. pp. 534-543, 2016.

[7] Mao, Chunyan, X. Liu, and T. Center. Integration analysis on the assembled frame of large forging hydraulic press. Forging & Stamping Technology (2016).

[8] Gui and Nan, An extension of hard-particle model for three-dimensional non-spherical particles: Mathematical formulation and validation. Applied Mathematical Modelling 40(4). pp. 2485-2499, 2016.

[9] Porteiro and Jacobo, Three-dimensional model of electrostatic precipitators for the estimation of their particle collection efficiency. Fuel Processing Technology 143. pp. 86-99, 2016.

[10] Jung and W. Kyung, Performance evaluation and optimization of a fluidized three-dimensional electrode reactor combining pre-exposed granular activated carbon as a moving particle electrode for greywater treatment. Separation & Purification Technology 156. pp. 414-423, 2015.

[11] Yang and Y. Tzu, Numerical simulation and optimization of turbulent nanofluids in a three-dimensional rectangular rib-grooved channel ☆. International Communications in Heat & Mass Transfer 66. pp. 71-79, 2015.

[12] Finney and A. Brad, Samsuhadi, and R. Willis. Quasi-Three-Dimensional Optimization Model of Jakarta Basin. Journal of Water Resources Planning & Management 118(1). pp. 18-31, 2014.

[13] Oyama and Akira, Aerodynamic Optimization of Three-dimensional Transonic Wing(Proceedings of the 15th NAL Symposium on Aircraft Computational Aerodynamics). Journal of Applied Remote Sensing9(1). pp. 095997-21, 2015.

[14] Zhao, Yingbo, G. Dong, and Y. Yang, Analysis and optimization of TSV–TSV coupling in three-dimensional integrated circuitsProject supported by the National Natural Science Foundation of China (No. 61334003). Journal of Semiconductors 36(4). 2015.

[15] R. E. González, PARAVT: Parallel Voronoi tessellation code .Astronomy and Computer 17. pp. 80-85, 2016.

[16] Rochepault, Etienne, G. Aubert, and P. Vedrine, Three-dimensional magnetic optimization of accelerator magnets using an analytic strip model. Journal of Applied Physics 116(2). pp. 023910-023917, 2014.